GAME OF BUDGETING AND HUMAN BEHAVIOUR

GAME OF BUDGETING AND HUMAN BEHAVIOUR

PRAKASH CHAND JAIN

CONCEPT PUBLISHING COMPANY, NEW DELHI-110059

The Indian Council of Social Science Research gave the financial support towards the publication of this work. However, the responsibility for the contents of the book - facts, opinions, conclusions, etc. - is entirely that of the author and not of the ICSSR.

ISBN 81-7022-245-1

First Published 1989

Published by
Ashok Kumar Mittal
Concept Publishing Company
A/15-16, Commercial Block, Mohan Garden
New Delhi-110059 (India)

Lesertypeset by
Microtech Advance Printing Systems (Pvt.) Ltd.
H-13, Bali Nagar,
New Delhi 110015

Printed by
New Gain Offset Printers
Shahjada Bagh
Delhi - 110035

CONTENTS

ABBREVIATIONS

B.M.	Budget Managers/Staff Managers
O.M.	Operating Managers/Budgetees/Line/Subordinates
Pvt.	Private Sector Company
Pbl.	Public Sector Company
S.D.	Standard Deviation
C.V.	Coefficient of Variation
P.E.	Performance Evaluation
P.A.	Performance Appraisal
J.S.	Job Satisfaction
J.P.	Job Performance
B.S.	Budget System
L.M.	Line Manager
S.M.	Staff Manager
Prod.	Productivity
Per.	Performance
N.S.	Not Significant

ACKNOWLEDGEMENTS

The present study was completed under the guidance and supervision of Professor L.S. Porwal and Professor P.K. Ghosh, Department of Commerce, University of Delhi.

I owe a deep sense of gratitude to Prof. L.S. Porwal, who initially stimulated me to take up the study of the game aspect of budget motivation and spared no pains in guiding me at all stages till I completed this work. Without his advice, encouragement and continuous help the thesis could not have been completed in time.

I also acknowledge my deep indebtedness to Prof. P.K. Ghosh whose guidance has prompted me intellectually in bringing together many of the core ideas that have emerged during the study. Further, his responses to the emerging ideas (pro and con) were helpful to me in the presentation of many vital issues with scientific precision.

I wish to express my sincere thanks to Prof. R.S. Nigam, Head, Department of Commerce, University of Delhi, for providing all the facilities necessary for conducting this study and giving me all possible encouragement.

I am thankful to my colleague, Dr. R.A. Yadav, for his enormous help in tightening our manuscript during the throes of final drafting to Shri Vinod Kumar, Sr. Lecturer in English, for his matchless care in editing and checking of our manuscript and improving its presentation, and to Shri N.M. Garg, Officer on Special Duty, for providing valuable help in my survey work.

Thanks are due to the authorities of Shri Ram College of Commerce for granting me study leave and other facilities to complete this study and University Grant Commission for providing financial assistance. I am also thankful to the staff of Delhi University Computer Centre and especially Mr. R.B. Garg, Senior Programmer, who not only developed the programme for Factor Analysis but also run it with personal interest in the shortest possible time. I also wish to thank the staff of Shri Ram College of Commerce and Ratan Tata Library for their co-operation.

I owe my thanks to the management of the Twenty Indian Companies for extending their co-operation in collecting the relevant data and two hundred and sixty nameless interviewees who willingly went through the stressful experience of long interviews.

I am also thankful to the Indian Council for Social Science Research for rendering the financial assistance for the publication of the work.

I thank Mr. Pradeep Kumar for typing the thesis with accuracy and on time.

This book is not dedicated to anyone. A dedication would be a poor compensation to Renu, Alok, Atul and Rahul, the four members of my family who carried the burden of its creation. They suffered under the tightness of their husband's and father's time budget without having participated in setting it. I hope that the completion of this book will restore the scope necessary for the game aspect in our lives.

PRAKASH CHAND JAIN

LIST OF TABLES

1

INTRODUCTION

1.1 IMPORTANCE OF THE PRESENT STUDY

The study of budgeting is important for three reasons. The first is a theoretical one: lack of conceptual clarity with respect to the usage of the term budgeting suggests the need for theoretical refinement of the concept. The other two reasons have a more pragmatic flavour. The study of budgeting is important because it provides a better understanding of how to improve the organisational effectiveness on the one hand and the quality of life of individual budgetees on the other. Let us consider each of the three reasons separately.

There is a need for understanding the concept of budgeting in unequivocal terms. Anthony(1) aptly describes the term budgeting as 'a process of planning the overall activity of the enterprise for a specific period of time, usually a year. An important objective of this process is to fit together the separate plans made for various segments of the enterprise so as to assure that these plans harmonise with one another and that the aggregate effect of all of them on the whole enterprise is satisfactory'.

Budgeting in a modern large corporation plays two basic roles. On the one hand, it is used as a management control device to implement policies which executives have decided upon, and to check achievements against established criteria. On the other hand, a budget is a device to determine feasible programmes. In either case, it tends to define - in advance - a set of fixed commitments and more importantly fixed expectations. Although budget can be flexible, it cannot help but result in the specification of a framework within which the firm will operate, evaluate its success and alter its programmes.

In its use as a general concept, scientific form, popular expression and cultural motif, budgeting has acquired a semantic richness (and confusion) attained by few words (ZBB, PPPB, MBO etc.) of corresponding significance in contemporary parlance(2). If one scans through the social science literature of the past three decades, one encounters numerous usages (Planning, Co-ordinating, Measuring, Controlling, Motivating etc.) of the concept of budgeting. In fact, the term budgeting has been used so often and in so many contexts that it has acquired an aura of equivocality.

As Seemans(3) pointed out, the concept of budgeting has been popularly adopted as the signature of the present epoch . It has been routine to define our troubles in the language of budgeting and to seek solution in those terms. But signatures are sometimes hard to read, sometimes spurious and sometimes too casually and promiscuously used. They ought to be examined with care. Similar concerns are expressed by Johnson(4), who characterises the concept of budgeting as being capable of carrying a great deal of feelings in an inexplicit, perplexing and deeply annoying way. Although in recent years, many psychologists and sociologists have attempted to demystify and operationalise the concept of budgeting as above but none of them seems to offer a scientifically organised and meaningful view of the concept that could have broad generality across culture. Lack of cross cultural generality of the existing conceptualisation of the phenomena has been discussed at some length in the subsequent paragraphs to follow. However, let us briefly mention it here to sensitise the issue.

Following Mayo, most social scientists and psychologists have viewed dysfunctional consequences of budgeting as resulting from the lack of opportunity within the budget system to satisfy budgetees' needs for personal growth, autonomy and self-actualisation. Modern budgeting with its bureaucratic structure, formal rules and regulations, impersonal character and mechanised routine operations, is accused of creating conditions for the loss of individuality that results in a state of a negative attitude towards budgeting. The need of the hour is to conceptualise budgeting in such a way that the attainment of budget standards will be its own rewards; that one should believe in the intrinsic aspects of budgeting; that one must value budget not because budget brings an external reward, but because is the best use of one's time and is intrinsically satisfying; and that budgetees should be engaged in 'for its own sake'. The operationalisation of the concept is based on these interpretations. The present conceptualisation of budgeting as a pressure device argues for a fresh look and reformulation of the term, that will have potential for high motivation and involvement of the budgetees in the budget system.

The second reason for the study of budgeting has its origin in the area of human resource management, where the persistent problem faced by managers is how to improve the organisational effectiveness through proper co-ordination of budgetees efforts. The effectiveness of any business organisation depends, in part, upon the perfection of the technical processes and equipments employed by it. Of atleast equal importance in a company's success is the full utilisation of human resources. Of particular significance in this regard is the co-ordination of efforts on the part of all budgetees in the organisation - from the office boy to the chief executive - to accomplish the purposes of the business.

A common complaint against budgeting in modern industry is that the drive towards such co-ordination of efforts is lacking, particularly at the level of rank and file budgetees. This short-coming according to many reveals itself most prominently in the failure of budgetees to make full use of their capacities in maintaining and raising the production standards. Such facts suggest the need for better understanding of the factors which stimulate the will to work and of the conditions or devices which can most effectively arouse or release these inner forces which lead the budgetee to participate willingly, fully and satisfying in furthering the aims of industry.

The final reason for the study of budgeting is to better appreciate the nature of budgetee's negative experiences in the budget system and how such experiences affect one's own life in general. The term budget is often used to describe the salient features of an individual's life experiences in contemporary society. For instance, the experience of dysfunctional attitudes towards budgets have been described in Jenkins(5) as a schizoid condition. Jenkins considers an alienated budgetee as one:

> "Who is subject to the stress of 'a threatening experience from which there is no physical scape', develops an elaborate protective mechanism; he becomes a mental observer, who looks on, detached and impassive at what his body is doing or what is being done to his body'. For that budgetee 'the world is a prison without bars, a concentration camp without barbed wire'. Instead of experiencing reality directly, he develops a 'false' self as a buffer for the real world, while the real self retires to an 'inner' position of unexposed safety. All of life seems full of 'futility, meaninglessness and purposelessness', since it is not, in fact being directly experienced. The real self is completely blocked, barred from any spontaneous expression or real freedom of action and totally sterile. In the absence of a spontaneous and natural creative relationship with the world which is free from anxiety, the 'inner-self' thus develops an overall sense of inner impoverishment, which is experienced in complaints of the emptiness, deadness, coldness, dryness, impotence, desolation, worthlessness of the inner life" (p. 43).

Like-wise, commenting on the life experience of an alienated factory budgetee, Tocqueville(6) observes that:

> "When a budgetee is unceasingly and exclusively engaged in the fabrication of one thing, he ultimately does his work with singular dexterity; but at the same time he loses the general faculty of applying his mind to the direction of work. He every day becomes more adroit and less industrious; so that it may be said of him, that in proportion as the workman improves the man is degraded..... When a budgetee has spent a considerable portion of his existence in this manner, his thoughts are forever set upon the object of his daily toil; his body has contracted certain fixed habits, which it can never shake off in a word, he no longer belongs to himself, but to the calling which he has chosen..... In proportion as the principle of technical aspects of budgeting is more extensively applied, the budgetees become more weak, more narrow minded and more dependent" (P -

190-91).

The excellence of budgeting is to be gauged not alone by a material yardstick, but also by the opportunities which it provides for the intellectual and emotional expression and the development of the budgetee. There is little merit in present budgeting which dulls the mind, warps the emotions, destroys the will and reduces the budgetee to an automation, even though sometimes it succeeds in providing an ever-increasing supply of material goods for distribution. For this reason it is not possible to think of the human element in budgeting in terms of productive efficiency alone, and therefore, there is an urgent need to take full account of the possible consequences of the present budget system and suggest measures which must be concerned with the satisfactions derived by the budgetee from the budget itself.

1.2 BEHAVIOURAL ASPECTS OF BUDGETING

In the early 1930's the management tenets of the behavioural school, also known as the human relations school, were brought to the fore. The theorists of this school were the first to question the underlying validity of the traditional tenets and therefore cast a shadow on the role of budgeting in the management process. This shadow lengthened as the human relations movement gained momentum and toward the end of 1950's it was evident that behaviouralists considered the budgeting process as an impediment to successful achievement of organisational objectives.

The behaviouralists viewed the organisation as a social system one in which a member's anxieties, tensions and conflicts were outide the understanding and control of the administrator. This people-oriented view was completely antithetical to the traditionalists work-oriented view. Behaviouralists saw the entity as he individual actions of the members, whereas the holistic concept f the early writers viewed the entity as a collectivity existing separate and distinct from the individual members.

Although still micro in its overall viewpoint, the behavioural school conceived the entity to be an integrated and self-contained social system. An Administrator could not simply organise the workplace in an efficient manner and as such equate people with physical resources. Rather, the primary task of the administrator was to choose resource arrangements that would most likely evoke a system of co-operative relationships. Individual and group feelings, perceptions, social values, harmony and morale comprised the anatomy of the administrative process. The viability of the organisation and the attainment of goals could only be achieved when an internal social equilibrium was reached where unproductive conflict was eliminated and co-operation reigned supreme.

Within this teamwork atmosphere, the traditional budgetary tool was a foreign matter. To postulate control of people as if they were things and force them to act within prescribed constraints violates the very nature of the human being. It was felt that the budgetary process failed to recognise that human behaviour is conditioned by personality as well as organisational factors and that the imposition of such restraints on human activity resulted in the dysfunctional actions so characteristic of our governmental bureaucracies. The natural reaction was that of conflict and rebellion against the organisation in general and the budget manager in particular because he personified the 'budgetary muzzle'.

1.3 BRIEF OVERVIEW OF THE WORK DONE

Few studies have been undertaken specifically on behavioural aspects of corporate budgeting. Some of them have been ad-hoc in nature covering one or two aspects of budgeting, in that the intent appears to have been data gathering and examination rather than exploring well-structured models and hypotheses. However, taken together, some very interesting lessons do emerge which provide a solid base for the present study. Some of the pertinent research works in the literature of budgeting and human behaviour are as follows:

ARGYRIS

Argyris(7) was the first behavioural scientist to express an interest in the nature and consequences of the budget process. From methodological point of view, this was a field study using open-ended interviews of line and staff supervisors in four medium-sized manufacturing organizations. The findings of the Study are: (a) budget pressure tends to unite the employees against management and tends to place the factory supervisors under tension. This tension may lead to inefficiency, aggression and perhaps a complete break-down on the part of the supervisors; (b) the finance staff can obtain feelings of success only by finding fault with factory personnel. These feelings of failure among factory supervisors led to many human relations problems; (c) the use of budgets as 'needlers' by top management tends to make the factory supervisors see only the problems of their own department. The supervisors are not concerned with other peoples' problems. They are not 'plant-centered' in outlook, and (d) supervisors use budgets as a way of expressing their own pattern of leadership. When these patterns result in people getting hurt, the budget, in itself becomes a neutral thing and often gets blamed.

To avoid these unfavourable reactions of budgetees, Argyris made two recommendations: First, the acceptance of budgets by genuine participation was crucial; and Second, accounting staffs needed to be trained in human relations.

These results seem to indicate that budgets are definitely disliked by the supervisors, foreman and the workers and thus the study elucidates only the negative aspect of budgeting and fails to divulge the positive possibilities for motivation inherent in the budget situation.

SIMON

Like the previous one, Simon's study(30) was also a field study using open-ended interviews of the line and staff managers. The study suggests that: (a) direct and active channels of person-to-person communication between line and staff are more important for management's use of figures that the way the figures themselves were presented; (b) it is highly desirable that account structures should be decentralised to industrial, manufacturing and sales units; (c) it is essential for the controller's department to develop direct and active channels of communication with line management ; and (d) development of staff and facilities for special studies are more important than elaboration of periodic accounting reports.

Simon's study was a quantitative one; it did not use 'counting,' 'measuring' and statistical validations. Also it did not start from prior hypotheses. However, the study produced a clear picture of the role of accounting staff in budget and cost control systems which tend to go fa: beyond mere 'technique'.

STEDRY

Stedry's(31) investigation was in the form of a laboratory experiment using university students as subjects preceded and followed by extensive mathematical model building. The study intended to measure the relationships between performance, aspiration levels and externally imposed budgets. Specific conclusions drawn from the study are: (a) low budgets were usually associated with very low performance; (b) implicit budgets, in general, were associated with good performance; (c) the influence of aspiration levels on performance varied depending on the budget level and on whether the aspiration levels were established before or after the budget was received; and finally, the combined result of each department concentrating on its own subunit goals do not necessarily lead to the best possible performance at the organisation level.

The findings of Stedry's work were based on laboratory experiments and the field experiments have been inconclusive. It is interesting to contrast Stedry's views on the nature of the budget process with the usual accounting view point which tends to ignore the behavioural traits of the individuals who are subject to the budget. Accountants will, no doubt, be reluctant to accept the notion that budgets must be custom-made for each individual, depending on his personality characteristics. But there is a good deal of evidence from motivation theory to suggest that such an approach may have a positive influence on performance and thus be desirable for the organisation.

HOFSTEDE

Hofstede(11) conducted a very comprehensive research study on motivational aspects of budget systems in six Dutch manufacturing companies. The key findings suggest that performance improves when: (a) budgetees participate in the setting of budget; (b) frequent communication about cost and budget variances between the budgetee and his boss; (c) budgetees knowing exactly which costs they are responsible for; and (d) frequent group meetings of the boss with his subordinates.

Though the study is very comprehensive, it is an exploratory one and, therefore, the findings of this study requires lot of experiments in different settings for generalisation.

DECOSTER AND FERTAKIS

The study of Decoster and Fertakis(32) is a field study involving 31 supervisors of manufacturing companies in U.S.A. The study suggests that: (a) a budgetee, when subject to induced budget pressure by his supervisor, tends to increase his own behaviour in both the dimensions of initiating structure and consideration; and (b) supervisors are aware that to become more effective they must encourage a higher effectiveness on the part of subordinates.

There is a need for replication of the study to see if the positive correlation between pressure and consideration is a consistent phenomenon. If it is so then there is a strong justification for re-examining the concept of budget motivation.

HOLSTRUM

Holstrum(33) conducted an experiment designed to measure and compare the effects of budget adaptiveness and budget tightness upon budgetee's responsiveness to random fluctuations and to environmental changes. The results of the experiment showed that: (a) there was no statistically significant difference in decision adaptiveness between groups differentiated according to either budget adaptiveness or budget tightness; (b) subjects working under tight budgets demonstrated a slightly higher adaptiveness than those operating under loose budgets; and (c) concerning possible interaction effects with ex-ente budgets, the tight budget group had the lowest adaptiveness index and the loose budget group the highest.

The research design of this study is subject to several limitations such as scope of the study, the nature of the subject, the experimental control procedures and the basic methodology. Since the scope of the experimental design included only imposed budgets, and only budgets for individuals, attempts to generalise the results to participative budget conditions or to budgets for groups or organisations would be questionable. Furthermore, the use of students as surrogates for business and industrial personnel may not have provided useful results(34).

SWIERINGA AND MONCUR

Swieringa and Moncur(17) designed a study to determine the budget-oriented behaviour of a sample of managers drawn from the branch organisation of large international bank related to various attitude, position, size and performance measures. It was concluded that: (a) managers exhibiting active participant behaviour have longer tenure and greater confidence in their organisation than the managers exhibiting involved exponent, reluctant victim or unconcerned recipient behaviour; (b) managers exhibiting active participant behaviour spend more time with subordinates and other managers but less time with customers than those managers exhibiting the other three aspects of budget-oriented behaviour. They appear also to experience considerably greater job-related tension; and (c) a branch bank manager's position and time in branch appear to be important variables with respect to his budget-oriented behaviour.

Some important omissions of the study are: (a) the study has failed to describe the organisation being investigated, particularly its policies on budgets and budgeting; (b) it also failed to review that we already know from behavioural sciences about the various issues discussed; and finally the study also failed to assist the reader in understanding and interpreting the results of methodologies that are essentially new to him.

CHERINGTON AND CHERINGTON

The study of Cherington and Cherington(35) presents the findings of an experiment involving 230 under-graduate students, both male and female to test the effects of budgetary control and reward contingencies on performance and satisfaction. The major conclusions are: (a) supervisor's leadership behaviour can influence worker's level of aspirations; (b) higher levels of aspirations are associated with higher subsequent performance; and (c) when rewards are budget-oriented there is less deviation from budget estimates, and when reward is only output-oriented, the budget estimates are less effective as controls on behaviour.

However, serious concerns are expressed by the researchers (36, 37) over various issues such as internal and external validity of the experiment, basic questions raised by the author, independent and dependent variables, task experimental control, data analysis, the choice of cross sections as well as appropriate and inappropriate rewards.

BRUNS AND WATERHOUSE

Like the previous one, it is a field study(19) involving twenty five organisations with diverse technologies. The major conclusions are : (a) high participation and perceived control were associated with structuring of activities; (b) size of organisation and technology was significantly & positively correlated with the structuring of activities; (c) those in highly structured organisations tended to perceive themselves as having more influence, they participate more in budget planning and they appear to be satisfied with budget related activities; and (d) managers in organisations where authority is concentrated were generally held accountable for fewer financial variables, experience superior-initiated pressure, see budgets as being less useful and limiting their flexibility, but they appear to be satisfied with the use of budgets by their superiors.

One possible implication of this study is that large process - dominated and technological organisations may not be as inhumane as they have been pictured in some places. For increased size and advanced process technology lead to or are atleast correlates with structuring of activities. Structuring implies distribution of authority and an increase in perceived control as well as increased participation in planning and feeling of involvement on the part of managers. Those who speak against large organisational units may be ignoring the countervailing tendency of size to lead to structuring of activities and greater job involvement.

FRANK COLLINS

In this study, Collins'(38) research problem was to determine how personality, perceived budget characteristics and attitudes toward these characteristics correlate with budgetary response attitudes. The study suggested that: (a) perceived budget characteristics, attitudes towards these characteristics and personal flexibility are important correlates, with budgetary response attitudes; and (b) increased age, tenure and status of organisation members did not correlate with increased budgetary responsiveness.

Since only one research instrument - a questionnaire - was used to measure the experimental variables, it is possible that this study is victim of certain common method errors which could have influenced the results. For example, it is possible that the halo effects could have contributed to the correlations between variables. Other common-method errors include the error of severity, error of leniency and the error of central tendency. Additionally, the research efforts reported here are concerned only with the correlationships among variables. It is not possible from these data to establish clear relationships between perceived budgetary characteristics and budgetary response attitudes.

IZZETIN KENIS

Kenis(18) examined some effects of budgetary goal characteristics such as participation, clarity, feedback, evaluation and difficulty on job related attitudes (job satisfaction, job involvement, job tension), budget related attitudes (attitude towards budget, budgetary motivation), and self-rated performance (budgetary performance, cost efficiency, job performance) for 169 department managers at the plant level who have budget responsibility. The results confirmed that: (a) budgetary participation and budget goal clarity tend to have positive and significant effects on job related and budget related attitude of managers; (b) participation and goal clarity, furthermore, were found to have significant influence on budgetary performance of managers; (c) high level of budget goal difficulty was found to have an adverse effect on attitudes and performance of managers; and (d) effects of budgetary evaluation and feedback on attitudes and performance of managers, on the other hand were found to be weak or insignificant.

The findings are subject to certain limitations, such as: (a) the scope of study is limited by its sample size, organisation level and industrial coverage; (b) response bias might have been arisen from the self-selection of the respondents; and (c) no mediating structural variables were included that may be capable of influencing the relationships.

MERCHANT

Merchant(21) investigates how differences in corporate level of budget systems are related to corporate size, diversity and degree of decentralisation; and how different choices in system design and uses are related to organisational performance and manager's motivation and attitudes. A model was developed from related findings in research in accounting and organisational behaviour, and the expectations in the model were explored with data gathered from 19 firms in the electronics industry. The results confirmed the hypotheses that: (a) budgeting as a part of the corporate control strategy, was related to the corporate context; (b) larger firms tended to make relatively high use of more formal administrative, as opposed to interpersonal controls; and (c) in all firms, the more formal and elaborate budgeting processes were generally received well by the managers, but in large firms they appear to be more positively linked with performance.

The findings should, however, be evaluated in the light of following observations. Firstly, the study does not present a totally general framework. It only covers middle level managers of the organisations. Second, the data may be biased due to self-selection of the sample of budgetees. Similarly, the managers surveyed were not randomly selected, and finally, some minor non-response bias may be present because only half of the managers responded to participate in the study.

BROWNELL

Brownell(39) examined the role of the personality variable, locus of control, as a moderator of the relationship between budgetary participation and managerial performance. The results of a laboratory experiment employing two separate subject groups - under graduate accounting students and managers from a large manufacturing company - revealed that: (a) a statistically significant interaction between participation and locus of control, affecting performance; and (b) budgetary participation was found to have a positive effect on individuals who feel that they have a larger degree of control over their destiny, while having a negative effect on those individuals who feel that their destinies were controlled by luck, chance or fate.

As the study is conducted in the laboratory setting choosing students as subjects, the generalization or external validity of the results will depend upon the extent to which all of the characteristics of the experimental setting replicate in the real world with the same degree of accuracy. In view of the surrogation of task, reward and situation, care should be exercised to avoid unqualified statements of applicability of the present results to a real setting. Bearing these observations in mind, however, it is possible to consider the implications of the results from two perspectives: job redesign and personnel management.

1.4 MAJOR DEFICIENCIES AND GAPS OF EARLIER STUDIES

From the studies described in the previous paragraphs it may be inferred that budgets are disliked by supervisors, foremen and the workers. However, the earlier studies do not present a comprehensive, systematic and clear picture of the impact of budget system on the budgetee's performance and job satisfaction. The major deficiencies and gaps of earlier studies are as follows:

First, present knowledge of budget's impact on budgetees' behaviour is incomplete which is due to lack of thorough and systematic attempt in this direction.

Second, conclusions of some of the studies discussed in the previous paragraphs are based on students as subjects in the laboratory experiments. Hence , there is an obvious need for field experiments in the organisational settings.

Third, some of the studies reported above have typically been micro in character and it is, therefore, difficult to generalise the findings of such studies beyond the individual company considered.

Fourth, since no such attempt has been made, worth its name, so far, in India and, therefore, Indian experience in this regard is almost nil.

Fifth, though the beneficial effects of budget system under certain conditions have been observed, but only in one study (11) which is exploratory in character, and hence, further confirmation of the findings of such study is required.

Finally, behavioural scientists have not translated their criticism into detailed prescriptions for the design of budget system and therefore, there is a need for a perfect budget system - perfect in the sense that high degree of goal-congruence is guaranteed.

FORMULATING THE PROBLEM FOR RESEARCH

Available literature on the subject reveals that budgets tend to make the employees feel dependent, passive, and subordinate to management. As a result, they experience pressure, interdepartmental strife, psychological failure, lack of control over their work environment, barrier to communication between the budget staff and the line people and pressure to be department-centered rather than organisation-centered. However, in practice a high level of motivation through budgets have been found to be associated with participation in the setting of budgets, frequent communication about cost and budget variances with the boss, knowing exactly which cost one is responsible for and frequent group meetings of the boss with subordinates.

The studies (8, 9, 30 and 31) on budgeting, which have been carried out by academics in recent years tend in varying degree to stress the accounting techniques and processes involved. At the other extreme, there are behavioural studies (7, 10, 11, 13, 17, 18, 21)dealing with the impact of budgets on people. The present study is an attempt to fill the gap between the two extremes by introducing the concept of play in the game of budget motivation. The problem posed is: How to live with the budgets and yet be motivated by them. On the basis of current thinking on the motivational implication of budgets, we may discuss two dimensions:

(a) The relevance of budget standards to the budgetee's task running from low to high. The word 'relevance' is used here and throughout the study in the sense of subjective or perceived relevance: as the budgetees see it.

(b) The attitude of budgetees towards the budget or standard system running from negative to positive.

The challenge now lies in identifying the possible conditions that can lead to both high relevance of budget standards and positive attitude of budgetees.

1.5 OBJECTIVES OF THE STUDY

The objectives of the present study are three folds:

(a) To record the opinion of budget managers and budgetees about the input factors which directly or indirectly affect the output of the budget system.

(b) To diagnose the main problems relating to the perceived characteristics of input factors of budget system; and

(c) To measure the contribution of the inputs of budget system to the final goals of an enterprise. The final goals, i.e., output of the budget system measured in this study are the motivations to all the employees for better performance (as a contribution to profitability) and the well being of budgetees of all ranks (as a contribution to job satisfaction).

1.6 OUTLINE OF THE STUDY

The present chapter is devoted to a general introduction to the subject of budgeting, its behavioural aspects, deficiencies and gaps of the earlier studies, statement of the problem and the objectives of the study. Chapter 2 describes the research design and methodology bearing on some of the variables of the theoretical model and the gross relationships among them. In Chapter 3, we have examined the more recent pertinent theories on budgeting in order to develop a conceptual framework for the present study which deals with the effects of budget control upon the budgetees' behaviour and their job performance. The brief overview of work done in recent years is also analytically presented in this chapter.

Chapter 4 forms the core of the study and empirically tests the theory on the basis of the survey of the research so as to the input output relationships of the budget system and to arrive at some conclusions. The impact of each input variable of budget system upon the job performance and job satisfaction of budgetees is described in Chapter 5. Chapter 6 deals with the demographic variables of budget managers and budgetees and impact of each demographic variable upon their attitude towards budget system as well as job performance and job satisfaction of budgetees. The impact of each organisational characteristic upon the attitude of budgetees and budget managers as well as job performance and job satisfaction of budgetees is summarized in Chapter 7. Finally, Chapter 8 presents the summary, conclusions, applicability of the study and some directions for future research.

2

RESEARCH DESIGN AND METHODOLOGY

This chapter describes the overall research design and methodology adopted to measure some of the variables in the theoretical model and to determine what gross relationships may exist among them. It contains two sections. Section 2.1 is devoted to the rationality of adopting a non-experimental research design, i.e., field study for the study. Section 2.2 describes the research methodology which is used for the overall research design chosen for the study. Selection of companies, sample of budgetees and budget managers, collection and processing of data and statistical tools employed for analysis are also presented in this section.

2.1 RESEARCH DESIGN

A field study is conducted in order to obtain budgetees and budget managers' budget-oriented behaviours that may influence the relevance of budget standards to the budgetees' task and attitude of budgetees toward budget standards. The reasons of designing a field study, i.e., non-experimental research design stem directly from the theoretical discussion presented in Chapter 3. Some of them are as follows:

First, a major implication of the theoretical model is the potential importance of conditions to ensure understanding of the effects of budgetary control on budgetees' behaviour and their performance. These conditions are inherent in the budget system and organisation setting in which budget control is used. Moreover the characteristics of the budgetees have equal impact on their behaviour. As these effects are highly interactive and inherently contextual, it is decided to conduct the study in the natural rather than controlled settings; this was expected to secure external validity of results to a greater extent than that of data from laboratory experiments as established by Cook & Compbell(12).

Second, this study is by necessity an exploratory one. It focuses on an area where little previous research has been done. Even though the discussion identifies some of the conditions surrounding the use of budget control, it does not assess the relative importance of these conditions for understanding the effects of its use on budgetees' behaviour. The field study is most appropriate, particularly for exploratory work because it helps in finding out the unknown variables in a given situation and what gross relationships may exist among them.

Third, in order to consider the possible significance of a large number of variables and to consider their possible effects on budgetees, the study is kept intensive rather than extensive. A field study makes it possible to cover large number of variables at a time and to study them intensively.

Finally, field experiment as a research design has also been widely used by Argyris(7), Fertakis(13), Hofstede(11), Schiff and Lewin(14), Onsi(15) and Hopwood(16) with more convincing results.

2.2 RESEARCH METHODOLOGY

In order to implement the overall research design discussed above, permission was requested with the chief executives or their close associates of each company to conduct a study on budgeting in their respective organisations. Two samples of budget managers and budgetees were drawn from each company and survey research questionnaires were used to obtain data from these managers. Along with this, personal discussions were held on various aspects of the budget system in the organisations to reconcile the ideas expressed in questionnaires. Data thus obtained were analysed with the help of statistical techniques and interpreted for practical suggestions.

2.2.1 *SELECTION OF COMPANIES FOR STUDY*

Companies for the study were decided on the following basis:

First, in order to maintain relatively close personal contact with the companies and their respondents, research sites were confined to the selected places in India.

Second, only the medium and large companies were considered for the study, in order to obtain relatively a large sample of managers from each company.

Third, to delimit the diversity of companies selected for research study is restricted to manufacturing companies only which were in the different industries or had different products, processes and markets.

Finally, to isolate some effects of budgetary control, the study is restricted to companies which tended to view the use of budgeting at a very advanced stage and of long standing (of atleast ten years) as an important tool of planning and control device, but which tended to use different amounts and forms of budgetary control.

In all, we have selected and given access to 25 companies both in private sector and public sector in the different industries. Out of 25, 20 companies were finally selected for the study whose responses were completed in all respects. In this study these companies will be referred as Pvt- 1, 2. 3, 4, 5, 6, 7, 8, 9, 10 for private sector companies and Pbl-1, 2, 3, 4, 5, 6, 7, 8, 9, 10 for public sector compaies. A brief description of these companies is presented in Table 2.1 given below.

2.2.2. *SAMPLE SELECTION*

Initially, it was decided to limit the number of budget managers to 100 and budgetees to 250 in the study. This number represented a compromise between aspirations and resources but was large enough to permit statistical analysis.

TABLE 2.1 **Corporate Characteristics of the Sample Companies**

S.N	Employees (N)	Turnover (in crores)	Market Dominance	Complexity	Technology	Autonomy of Operations
Pvt-1	9000	250	National	Diversified	One of the best	Substantial
2	13000	196	National	Diversified	One of the best	Substantial
3	16000	250	National	Related	One of the best	Substantial
4	6000	150	None	Diversified	Average	Substantial
5	4600	400	Inter-National	Diversified	Best	Full
6	1500	25	National	Single	Above Average	Full
7	1200	80	National	Diversified	Best	Substantial
8	3000	1300	Inter-National	Diversified	Above Average	Full
9	1582	120	Inter-National	Single	Above Average	Full
10	9000	50	National	Single	Average	Full
Pbl-1	6000	200	National	Single	Best	Substantial
2	4524	370	National	Single	Best	Substantial
3	200000	3000	National	Single	Best	Full
4	13800	247	National	Related	Best	Substantial
5	72000	1302	National	Related	Best	Full
6	15000	1338	National	Single	Best	Full
7	3000	40	National	Single	Average	Substantial
8	9000	1100	National	Single	Average	Substantial
9	6500	106	National	Single	Above Average	Substantial
10	6000	400	National	Single	Above Average	Substantial

In each Company, 5 budget managers (in some companies designated as financial manager, financial advisor, Vice-President Finance or director finance or executives associated with the development & execution of budget system) as well as 10 budgetees (mostly from middle level operational and marketing managers) were selected depending upon the size and nature of the organisation. These interviewees were directly associated with the development and implementation of the budget system. The identification of the respondents usually occurred while the chief executive or his close associate was explaining the organisation chart of the company concerned. Our original plan was to select a random sample from all employees in each organisation proved unfeasible because organisations were reluctant or unable to make complete list available to us. Table 2.2 given below presents the profile of respondents.

TABLE 2.2 **Demographic Characteristics of Budget Managers and Budgetees**

Demographic Characteristics	Nature of Respondents		
	Budget Managers	Line Managers	Total
Potential Number of Respondents	100	200	300
Number of Respondents Obtained	97	163	260
Number of Respondents Obtained (%)	97 %	82 %	87 %
Average Age (in years)	44.8	39.6	41.5
Seniority in Organisation (in years)	5.47	5.52	5.49
Seniority in Position (in years)	4.36	3.97	3.57
Seniority in Budgeting (in years)	17.7	4.67	10.50
Educational Level (Above graduation)	82.7 %	64.5 %	73.10 %

Table 2.2 shows that a somewhat higher percentage of budget managers responded to the questionnaire instrument than did those in other departments (Budgetees). This is probably due to relatively higher educational level of the budget managers and their consequent ability and willingness to deal with written material. Table 2.2 also shows a very little difference between the two managerial group of respondents in either average age or average seniority but a wider gap can, however, be noticed regarding the association with the budget system of the organisations. This can be interpreted as that staff officers mostly remain stick to one line of work for a longer period as compared to the line officers who frequently change their jobs.

2.2.3 *DATA COLLECTION*

Data for the study were collected mainly through questionnaires, interviews and company records. The procedure adopted is as follows:

First, the research procedure included a half an hour to one hour interview with the chief executive or a close associate in each organisation. The interview time was spent in explaining the general nature of the study, the importance attached to the co-operation of each executive and identifying a sample of budget managers and budgetees who are directly involved in developing or executing the budget system of the organisation.

Second, the chief executive called on telephone or sometime wrote to each budget manager and budgetee informing them that they had been chosen to participate in a research study on budgeting. He also informed that they would be receiving materials which would explain the nature of the study and their limited involvement in it. This call further stated that their participation is earnestly needed to make the study successful and meaningful. Moreover, he assured them that their responses would be held in complete confidence by the researcher and they would be sent a summary report of the final results.

Third, we had a programme for seven days to study each company and to get first hand information through questionnaires and personal interviews. During the visit, a survey research questionnaire was given to each participant separately along with a covering letter to get them acquainted with the objective and procedure of the study.

Fourth, each respondent was requested to complete the questionnaire within a relatively short period of time without discussing the contents of the questionnaire with his colleagues because they may or may not be participating in the study. This request was made to seek the unbiased opinion of the interviewees.

Fifth, separate questionnaires were prepared for the budgetees and budget managers. A brief summary of the contents of the questionnaires is as follows: Questionnaire for budgetees is consisting of the following seven parts.

Part I is concerned with general information about the interviewee's demographic variables, such as, interviewee's age, education, years of working in company, present position and association with budget system of the company.

Part II refers to the corporate characteristics such as nature of the company, major products, turnover, number of employees, market position, complexities of activities, technology, profit centres, management philosophies towards delegation of authority and corporate objectives.

Part III is the core of the questionnaire which seeks the opinions of the budgetees toward perceived budgetary characteristics such as budgetary goals, participation in budget setting, superior-subordinate relationships, evaluation and reporting of budgetary performance, role of line and staff in budget development, follow up and corrective action and cultural and personality characteristics of the budgetees. For this, a 46-item questionnaire was developed and used to measure budgetees' budget oriented behaviour towards above characteristics. These variables were heavily drawn from the existing body of psychological and organisational test instruments based on the characteristics of our sample and also on the research finding of Argyris(7), Fertakis(13), Hofstede(11), Onsi(15), Swieringa and Moncur(17), Kennis(18), Bruce Irvine(9), Bruns and Waterhouse(19), Macintosh(20) and Merchant(21). The remaining questions are based on the experience of pilot study conducted by the researcher.

Part IV seeks the attitude of budgetees toward budget system. Budget-oriented attitude toward budget control was operationally defined as the predisposition to support or withhold support of the budget and even to sabotage the budget. Important facets of this predisposition are budgetees' ego-identification, general willingness to strive to attain the budgeted performance, to induce and encourage budgetary performance, and willingness to support the budgetary process. These variables were successfully tested in the studies of Swieringa and Moncur(17), Bruns and Waterhouse(19) and Hofstede(11).

Part V explains a self-rating of overall performance of the budgetees, by asking them to rate their department on a scale from 'always' to 'never'. The respondents were also asked to rate the cost efficiency of their departments and their overall job performance. A subjective performance measure was necessary because it is almost impossible to get properly matching data in a cross organisational study. Self-ratings were used not only because they were relatively easy to gather, but also because of recent evidence. Heneman(22) suggested that self-ratings may be more accurate and precise than superiors ratings. He also suggested that this is credible because superiors' are typically less well informed and more subject to hallow effect.

Part VI deals with the extent to which budget control affects the manager's intrinsic motivation. This was measured with a three-item Hackman and Porter(23) Scale, later used by Dermer(24) and Hofstede(11). The managers were asked to indicate their agreement on a scale from 'always' to 'never', with statements linking achievements of budgetary goals to the feelings of personal satisfaction, accomplishment, growth and development.

Part VII refers to an independent questionnaire which mainly covers the tight or looseness of budget standards, clarity of budgetary goals, authority of overall development of the budget, involvement of budgetees, internal and external factors influencing the budgeted efficiency, actual and desirable role of the budgetees in the budget setting, budgetary information system, interaction between superior and subordinates, evaluating and reporting of budget performance. These issues were discussed personally with the concerned executives. This strategy allowed an interview which was relatively relaxed and unstructured, so that exploratory work could be carried out with more confidence and trust.

The similar type of questionnaires were also made available to budget managers except that the statements were different. Table 2.3 summarizes the data about the number of questionnaires distributed to and returned by both budgetees and budget managers.

2.2.4 *DATA PROCESSING AND TOOLS OF ANALYSIS*

Data were analysed with the help of computer IBM-360 of Delhi University.

The study covers 46 variables for budgetees and 47 for budget managers. The responses on the variables were obtained on the Likert-Scale from 'always' to 'never'. Observed variables were analysed with the help of statistical techniques known as averages, standard deviation, correlation and factor analysis.

Averages of the total scores on each variable were calculated to get one single value that describes the characteristic of the entire mass of unwieldly data. As averages alone cannot describe the pattern of a set of observations adequately unless all the observations are the same, the variability of the variables around the mean was further investigated. To know the pattern of relations existed among the variables, Karlpearson's coefficient of correlation was calculated. This technique was adopted because: (a) it is based on relative measures of co-variance; (b) algebraic sign of Pearson's coefficients of correlation indicates the direction and magnitude of relationships between the two variables; and (c) lies between ± 1.

To identify these major patterns, the correlations were further analysed by a technique known as factor analysis. It reduces the large number of variables (i.e.. 46 & 47) to a smaller number of variables by describing each, linearly in terms of (n) new uncorrelated factors. These factors provide a parsimonious description of the observed data by retaining the most important information contained in the original data. The factor model extracts the maximum variance of the data explainable by the underlying factors that describe the structure and pattern of original variables (see Herman for more details).

Within this strategy, the variables entered the factor model without specifying the grouping of the variables into any a-priori structure. These correlations were factorially analysed by the principal axes method developed by Harman(25). This technique is useful to map the empirical concepts of a domain, reduce data to a smaller set of independent variables and test hypotheses about major sources of covariation. The communalities were estimated by the highest correlation for a variable as favoured by Thurstone(26).

TABLE 2.3 **Summary Data about Questionnaires Distributed to and Returned by Budget Managers and Budgetees**

Company	Budget Manager			Budgetees			Total		
	Distri-buted	Retur-ned	Percen tage	Distri-buted	Retur ned	Percen-tage	Distri-buted	Retur-ned	Percen-tage
PVT- 1	5	5	100	10	9	90	15	14	93
2	5	5	100	10	7	70	15	12	80
3	5	5	100	10	9	90	15	14	93
4	5	5	100	10	8	80	15	13	87
5	5	5	100	10	9	90	15	14	93
6	5	4	80	10	6	60	15	10	67
7	5	4	80	10	7	70	15	11	73
8	5	5	100	10	8	80	15	13	87
9	5	5	100	10	8	80	15	13	87
10	5	5	100	10	7	70	15	12	80
PBL- 1	5	5	100	10	8	80	15	13	87
2	5	5	100	10	8	80	15	13	87
3	5	5	100	10	10	100	15	15	100
4	5	5	100	10	9	90	15	14	93
5	5	5	100	10	9	90	15	14	93
6	5	5	100	10	9	90	15	14	93
7	5	4	80	10	7	70	15	11	73
8	5	5	100	10	10	100	15	15	100
9	5	5	100	10	7	70	15	12	80
10	5	5	100	10	8	80	15	13	87
TOTAL	100	97	97	200	163	82	300	260	87

The number of factors were determined on the basis of eigen-values equal to or greater than one. The eigenvalues measure the variance accounted for by a factor. This criteria assumes that the factors extracted define a certain level of variance among the variables. Since the variance of variable is unity, the cut-off rule rejects factors that do not account for atleast the variance of one variable. These factors were further rotated by using the orthogonal varimax criteria [Harman(25), Haris(27), Kaiser(28), and Warbuston(29)] to make factorial technique to be more adequate to define the minimum dimensionality of the data and a basis of the space. A strong feature of varimax is its ability to discern the same cluster of variables regardless of the number and combination of other variables in the analysis (28) and finally variables with a loading .40 or greater as a factor were selected as the factor's domain (11, 15 and 18). Variables loading on each factor and factor loading coefficients were used to develop descriptive names.

3

BUDGETING: A THEORETICAL FRAMEWORK

This chapter is devoted to the overall theoretical framework for the study. It contains three sections. Section one describes the definition and scope of corporate budgeting, assumptions about human behaviour on which accounting theory of budgeting is based, impact of budgets on budgetees' behaviour and finally reasons of failure of present budgetary practices in attaining corporate objectives. Section two deals with the meaning and characteristics of the game, conditions for creating game-spirit and playing the game of budgeting. Failing access to any broad based and systematic studies on budgetees' behaviour under different budgeting arrangements, section third is largely devoted to psychological studies which are more or less germane to the topic of our study.

3.1 ACCOUNTING THEORY OF BUDGETING A PRESSURE & DEVICE

The accounting system and budget system both are built around the same organisational structure, and both are information systems concerned with the same operations and financial situations. Accounting reports quantify information on historical events and conditions; the budget reflects what those values were expected to be, and what is expected in future. Following paragraphs throw some light on various aspects of the accounting theory of budgeting in practice.

3.1.1 *BUDGET: DEFINITION AND SCOPE*

Budgeting has been defined in many ways. Just to remove or atleast mitigate some of the ambiguity which may result from the usage of the term budget in this thesis, an attempt has been made to relate it to the definitions in common use. The most comprehensive use of the term is exemplified in the following definition of budgeting by Eric Kohler(40) as under:

1. A financial plan serving as a pattern for and a control over future operations;
2. hence, any estimate of future costs; and
3. a systematic plan for the utilization of man power, material or other resources (p.75).

Implicit in Kohler's definition is the existence of a multiplicity of purposes for which budgets are constructed. Although different writers and practitioners put different stresses, there is common agreement that budget is a tool of management control to facilitate the achievement of business goals. Budgets are primarily intended to yield the following results, which may be regarded as goals or constraints for the business:

1. Higher profitability by co-ordinating efforts, avoiding waste and improving the quality of management decisions; and
2. Optimal liquidity and the best way of financing the business with advance knowledge of cash needs.

These purposes can be achieved through budgets in various ways. A Dutch Standard text book on budgeting (41) lists the following four basic functions of a budget to attain the above objectives: (a) authorising, (b) forecasting, (c) planning, and (d) measuring. Stating in the language of organisation theory, budgeting is a method of translating the goals of the organisation, into operational terms; disseminating these goals to the appropriate decision-makers; and facilitating, co-ordinating and controlling the actions of the various sub-units within the organisation. A recent accounting text (42) describes the following principal steps of budgetary control process followed by most organisations:

1. Preparation of the plan consistent with the goal of the business.

2. Review, discussion and adjustment of the plan as needed to facilitate its accomplishment.
3. Communication of sub-sections of the plan to responsibility centres within the organisation.
4. Comparison of actual performance with planned results.
5. Analysis and explanation of variances from the plan.
6. Corrective actions where significant unfavourable variances occur between planned and actual performance.

3.1.2 *ASSUMPTIONS ABOUT HUMAN BEHAVIOUR IN THE ACCOUNTING THEORY OF BUDGETING*

The accounting theory of budgeting as described above, take certain human reactions for granted. Budgets are intended to control the behaviour of people that of the budgetees and managers who are responsible for implementing the budget. The accounting theory of budgeting is based on the belief that budgets and cost standards act as incentives for motivating the budgetees. Taking a closer look at what accountants write about budgets, one can find a number of assumptions about human behaviour. Some of which are as follows:

1. The authority of control lies at the top of the organisation and the control lines flow from the top downward.
2. The relationship of lower levels to higher levels of management in the organisation can meaningfully be described in terms of accountability (43).
3. Goal setting by the organisation improves peoples' performance.
4. Having people participate in goal-setting improves their performance still more.
5. Managers will initiate action when a deviation of actual situation from the standard is reported to them.
6. The perfect manager manages by exception.
7. People react to control systems as individuals.

There is ample evidence to illustrate management's use of budgeting as a pressure device to increase productive efficiency. The research findings of Youmann(44), Moore(45), and Argyris and Miller(46) corroborate the hypothesis. In a study of four organisations made by Argyris and Miller the majority of the managers interviewed felt that employees were basically lazy, has no desire to work and had to be pressurised and needled. Some comments made by top management officials in interviews revealed that these beliefs were not completely unfounded.

For example:

> 'I will tell you my honest opinion. About 5% of the people work, 10% of the people think that they work, and other 85% would rather die than work'.
>
> 'I think there is a definite need for more pressure. People need to be needled a bit. Man is inherently lazy, and if we could only increase that pressure, I think the budget system would be more effective'.
>
> 'There are lots of workers... who don't have the capacity to do things other than what they are doing.... they are lazy.... they don't have the desire'.
>
> 'Nine-tenths of the employees have no goals, and they don't give a damn, and they are glad not to have a goal. It is the same all over, in your plant or anywhere. People got to be pressurized-needled. I don't mean you have to hit them over the head with a hammer. Just keep them needling' (47, p.22-27).

The same attitudes were expressed in a dramatic fashion by one executive who said:

> 'the majority of workers are good natured slobs who want to be left alone in routine jobs ......'
>
> 'thousands resist promotion because they do not want to be lifted out of a rut' (47, p.3).

The spontaneous conversations of a top management group trying to understand effective leadership in an industry concluded:

> 'The chief executive in a company like our own is responsible for the team and the way the team plays' (48, p.45).

Another executive added:

> 'our past president was guiding a group to sound decisions. However, there was never any question as to where the head of the table was' (48, p.45).

Still another stated:

> 'the president cannot afford to concern himself with smoothing out the relations because he would then be just a 'mopper-upper' and would not fulfil his duty of staying out of current operations and concerning himself with future plans' (48, p.46).

Even when the top executive asked questions, then impact seemed to be needling, stimulating.

> 'Ask him the things that will help him-or scare him; or stimulating him-to do his job right. You have to ask questions that will cause him not to be complacent, but to consider his whole activities broadly. By less checking and more asking you show confidence in the operating manager. He will like it a lot better and he will work a lot harder' (48, p.69).

These conversations with top management reveal how budgeting is practised. It is the executive who plans, who is responsible, who is at the head of the table, who guides and reconciles points of view, who makes decisions, who asks questions to stimulate, scare and motivate the subordinates to work harder, who gives confidence, provides information and arouses interest.

An insightful top executive summarized the reasons as to why it was easy for the executive to fall into the directive pattern of budgeting:

> 'As an executive, you don't realise until you look at yourself how much you take for granted the fact that when someone comes into your office to make a complaint or express himself, sooner or later you are dominating the conversation. You are in your office because you have an ability to dominate conversation. You have been chosen for your managerial place because you may be

> little more skillful in winning out in verbal fisticuffs with your associates, the people who are below you or on the same level with you. If that is true, unconsciously then, you are going to impose what you think is the right approach to a problem upon the person. And he or she is going to leave the office completely dissatisfied with the result of the conversation, but you are going to say, "We keep an open door in this plant, and anybody can come in and talk to me". In my own view point I hope none of you will think that I am completely irrelevant on this - I think the myth of the open door, so far as industrial and commercial management is concerned, is one of the worst plagues with which we have cursed ourselves. We think that simply because we say to people, 'You can always come and talk to us', that they will. They are not going to come in and talk to us, because of our symbols of authority. Again, as all of us know, the higher you get up the ladder, the less likely you are to get real expressions of what individuals are thinking' (49, p.6-7).

Hodges(50) basing his comments on Rathe's analysis of budget controls observed that the basic budget activities were as follows. First, management should determine the overall plan. Included in this activity are such sub-activities as 'the design of the specific programme' (including the policies and plans), and 'the development of tools' such as 'organisation', 'systems', 'procedures', 'methods', and 'standards'. Second, management must control and determine what actually takes place. Are the plans followed according to definition and are the tools used as suggested? In order to answer questions like these, data must be obtained for management to evaluate. Martin(49) made the same point when he stated, 'the operator is not only to be told 'what to do', but also 'how to do it', and 'what equipment' to use. This means jobs are planned in detail and comprehensive instructions are issued so that the operator will perform the job in accordance with the plan.

3.1.3 *IMPACT OF BUDGETS ON BUDGETEES' BEHAVIOUR*

What impact will such budgets tend to have upon the budgetees' behaviour? First, the budget consists of a set of specific goals and gives the appearance of inflexibility. There is little room for manipulation or escape if results are not going to turn as expected. Given the nature of budgets, the budgetees feel that they are working under pressure and that the budget is the principal instrument of pressure. In a famous study, Argyris(7) reported that management control, such as budgets, were definitely disliked by the budgetees. For example:

> 'I am violently against the figures. I keep away from showing them to the workers. I know my boys are doing a good job. They are trying to do their best. If I give them the heat with this stuff, they will blow their top' (p.10).

Another operating manager stated:

> 'You cannot use budgets with people. Just can't do anything like that. People have to be handled carefully and in our plant, carefully does not mean with budgets. Besides, I don't think my people are lazy' (p.10).

Finance people also admit of the attitude that budgets help 'keep employees on the ball' by raising their goals and increasing their motivation. Argyris(7) provided the following examples of how accountants saw budgets as a means of putting pressure on operating managers:

> 'The important thing for us to do is follow up. The supervisor's interest lags unless someone is constantly checking up on him. A little pressure. If you don't, the tendency is to lag. You can't blame supervisors. They are interested in their machines' (p.6).

But what type of pressure did they have in mind?

> 'as soon as we examine the budget results and see a fellow is slipping, we immediately call the factory manager and point out, 'Look Joe, you are behind your budget. What do you expect to do about it?' True, he may be batting his brains out already on the problem, but our phone call adds a little more pressure - er - well, you know. We let them know we are interested' (p.6).

Increase in pressure is expressed somewhere in the new budget in term of a 'tighter' figure. Due to this, tension begins to mount. People become uneasy and suspicious. Management keep the informal pressure to keep production at the new level. Any new increase will have to be 'paid for' by management in 'free' tickets to football games, slowdowns, strikes etc (50). Finally this constant increase in pressure from top management for greater production leads to long term negative results. People living under these conditions tend to become suspicious of every new move management makes to increase production, particularly budgets.

Budgeting also produces unwanted side effects (8, 9, 10, 51). One of these is the formation of small informal groups to combat pressure and reduce tension. Such informal groups usually have their own goals, and such goals conflict with those of the organisation. Pressure is most accute on supervisors who are compelled to accept responsibility for meeting budget goals. In addition to forming informal groups, they try to shift responsibility to other departments or to question the validity of the budgeted data. Such a situation makes it difficult for the accounting staff to discharge their responsibilities effectively.

It was further noticed that some times supervisors distort successfully the measurement process. This is done by overt manipulation of the data or by actions which improve his immediate performance but harm the firm in the long run; for example, a foreman delays, needed maintenance.

A third undesirable side effect was observed from the budgeting process, viz., the overemphasis on departmental performance as compared with the firm's performance. Important inter-departmental dependencies and economies were ignored or overlooked in a quest for optimisation of the department's performance.

A fourth effect was perhaps, the undue publicity given to individual's performance, particularly the aspects of failure. The extensive exposure given to performance reports across departments for comparative purpose increased friction among supervisors as well as between supervisors and the accounting staff.

Finally and particularly a noxious consequence of the budget and performance evaluation process is the stifling of initiative. Individuals are often discouraged from trying something new when the established ways have a large chance of success and new methods portend a greater degree of uncertainty.

Abruzzi(52) confirms the conclusion that the budgetees 'cheat' and 'distort' their production record in order to make the record look the way they believe is in their interest. He noted that this behaviour prompts one to question the validity of the resultant production standards.

Jasinski(53) in his analysis of the impact of budgetary controls presents evidence that budgetees fudge the records to serve their own interests. He also concluded that as a result of budgets, inter-departmental conflicts arise (supervisors blaming each other for waste and errors), production and maintenance costs are increased which in turn results in impairment of quality and irregular output. All of these lead to much waste of the executives time.

Argyris in an analysis of the impact of budgetary controls showed that budgetees feel the pinch of budget when the planning part (and all its aspects) is taken up by top management and they are left primarily with the responsibilities to perform. In such cases, budgetees are assigned highly fractionised and specialised jobs from the performance of which they derive little satisfaction. Moreover, denied of participation in the planning aspects of budgets, the budgetees are deprived of an opportunity to participate in important decisions affecting their working life. They feel a loss of control over their work world; and these conditions tend to be disliked by mature individuals. Finally, the lack of participation in defining the goals will cause the budgetees to feel psychological failure.

In brief, budgets tend to make the employees feel dependent, passive and subordinate to management. As a result of budgets, they experience pressure, inter-departmental strife, psychological failure, lack of control over their work environment, communication barriers between the budget people and line people and pressure to be department-centred rather than organisation centered.

3.1.4 *WHY BUDGETING GOES WRONG*

Since budgeting for cost control seems such an obvious need, what then goes wrong? Sometimes the most obvious symptoms of trouble are repeatedly overlooked. Management develop characteristic defences and responses, and fail to recognise these symptoms as conflict indicators. The following exclamations are common in organisations:

> 'But it will work if they would only give it half a chance'.
>
> 'If only they would listen to me'.
>
> 'There is nothing wrong with the budget.....'
>
> 'Everything is run by the accountants' (54, p.355).

These kinds of statements signify basic problems. They are indicative of serious gaps in the development of internal organisational system. They cry for managerial response. It is unfortunate that management fail to recognise signals which cause companies to permit many inherently fine budget systems to deteriorate badly. In fact, some have deteriorated so badly that they do more harm than good. At the same time, management permit the roots of conflict, frustration and discontent to grow deeper, and to become more firmly implanted in the bedrock attitudes of the firm (55). Human and mechanical problems give rise to possibilities of dysfunctional consequences with the result that some functional objectives become difficult, if not impossible, to attain.

Almost invariably, the failure of a budget system is the result of management's inability to recognise the human relations problem inherent in the budget system as in any other control system. It is important to realise that budgetees have certain needs which condition their own objectives.

1. They seek compensation for their work which will enable them to provide some desired standard of material welfare for themselves and their families.
2. They need an outlet for the physical and intellectual energies which will provide both stimulation and satisfaction.
3. They seek self-realisation - a sense of worth and usefulness.
4. They are inclined to pursue further growth and greater personal effectiveness.

5. They seek the recognition of fellow workers, no matter what their organisational status is.
6. They cherish identification with a worth-while and successful undertaking (56, p.305-6).

In this context, budgeting is given an interpretation in our study which is sharper than the one cited above. The objective of budgeting should be to increase long-run performance of the enterprise at the fastest possible rate through the optimum utilisation of human resources and well being of the people in the system. For the moment at least, the question of just what rate is the fastest possible will be overlooked in order to devote attention to the word budgeting in terms of gamesmanship and a brief description of its implications which follows.

3.2 BUDGETING IN GAME THEORY - THE GAME SPIRIT

The link between problems of budgeting in complex organisations and game theory is that they have a common interest in the design of self-monitoring system. The budget system for complex organisations cannot be entirely regulated from outside; they must rely on some degree of self-regulations (57). As the complexity and uncertainties of the budget multiply, the greater is the need for the budget to incorporate self-adaptive elements.

A somewhat similar point is made by Shillinglaw(58) in the course of some discerning remarks on budgets. The need for delegating responsibility in an organisation of any size leads to the presumption that a good budget should rely heavily on self-correction. This in turn involves certain implicit assumptions: that budgetary targets are sufficiently demanding to call forth strong efforts by those whom they are supposed to control, and that the latter are adeqately motivated meet the targets, the motivation being supplied by the entire reward structure of the firm. It seems more realistic to suppose, however, that the typical situation we are likely to be concerned with is that of a co-operative game situation (59).

'Co-operative game is a self monitoring hence-stable-mechanism in which everyone can see that any betrayal will do more harm to the betrayer than it will do him good' (60).

Budgeting and budgetary control with full and genuine participation in the setting of the budgets might approximate to this situation, though in practice participation more often tends to be pseudo-participation. Perhaps a closer counterpart would be a firm where all employees were imbued with the 'the game spirit', as described by Hofstede(11). This spirit has also been observed in the theory of teams (61). Having described the similarities between game theory and budget systems in use, further probe in this direction is made in the following paragraphs.

3.2.1 *GAME: MEANING AND CHARACTERISTICS*

To avoid the misunderstanding about the term 'Play' or 'Game' arising out of various interpretations, it is appropriate to adopt a comprehensive definition given by Drever(62), in the Dictionary of Psychology:

> 'Play: activity, physical or mental existing apparently for its own sake, or having for the individual as its main aim in the pleasure which the activity itself yields (p.211).
>
> Game: organised play according to definite rules with a definite objective and usually competitive' (p.103).

The idea of 'play' and 'game' given in the above definition is basically different from the Mathematical Theory of Games which postulates that the players are completely rational and deal with the process of playing (63). It is also different from 'Transactional Games' which deal with the games that are irrational, and hence more real(64). The clever gamesmanship in Stephen Potter's(65) sense is often a poor strategist and eventual loser. Our concern in this study is not with the gamesmanship but with a game of potential players for definite achievements of desired results.

Several writers (11, 66, 67, 68, 69, 70) have given their opinions about the motivational aspect of game. These studies are not sufficient in themselves in giving a very comprehensive view of it. However, Huizinga(69) attempted to give a very compact idea systematically. Some of the main characteristics of the game according to him are as follows:

- Play is an activity carried out for its own sake (66).
- It has a potential for high motivation (70) and involvement of the players (71).
- It entails a challenge for definite achievements (67).
- It pre-supposes a certain free area to play-in, a certain 'margin', 'scope' or 'play', both in 'time' and 'space' (69).
- It is separated from real life (72).
- It follows certain rules, which are voluntarily accepted by the players and conscientiously followed (72).
- It has a potential for creating a teamspirit.
- Absence of compulsion (69).

Summing up the formal characteristics of play, we might call it a free activity standing quite consciously outside 'ordinary' life as being 'not serious', but at the same time absorbing the player intensely and utterly. It proceeds within its own boundaries of 'time' and 'space' according to fixed rules and in an orderly manner. It promotes the formation of social groups which work for definite achievements.

3.2.2 *CONDITIONS OF GAME SPIRIT*

The characteristics of game explained above show that there is every possibility of invoking the game-spirit under certain conditions. The most important condition of game is that it is played 'for its own sake' or 'for the sake of pleasure'. Secondly, the incorporation of 'margin', 'scope', or 'play' element to maintain control-autonomy-balance, and lastly, if any situation arises out of conflict because of competition among players resolve that by bargaining in standard setting. These conditions are discussed hereunder:

First, when it is said that playful activities are 'for its own sake' or 'for the sake of pleasure', this means partly that the players show little sign of strain and, above all no biologically important consequences appear to hinge on them.

The picture of play as a type of action in which an organism indulges and derives pleasure from performing it has been encouraged by Buhler's(73) concept of 'functional pleasure'. However, it is clear in the later part of the study that there is more to play than this.

Nevertheless, whether an organism plays, and if so, in what form, depends on its motivational condition, which calls for study. Secondly, while the organism might very well begin by carrying out in a random order, a number of actions that happen to be pleasurable, selection and learning make for their re-appearance very soon.

Selective learning necessitates some kinds of feedback to reinforce some forms of behaviour and extinguish others through non-reinforcement. If reinforcement does not come from some consequences effected in the external environment, it must come from some inner consequences and in particular from the central nervous system. When we say that play or some other activity is engaged in 'for its own sake', what we really mean is that it is engaged in only when the organism is in the kind of motivational conditions that makes these inner consequences rewarding. Behaviour of this kind, is what we call 'intrinsically motivated' (74).

This behaviour flourishes best in the absence of compulsion. The same is true of play. Although one might compel a child to play against his will, the game will straightaway lose one of the characteristics that makes it play. As Huizinga(69) wrote:

> 'Play to order is no longer play; it could at best be, but a forcible imitation of it. By this quality of freedom alone, play makes itself off from the course of the natural process' (p.26).

Another pre-condition to achieve the above environment of gamesmanship require the presence of certain free area to 'play' with a certain 'margin', or 'scope' or 'play', both in 'time' and 'space'. Many researchers have investigated the motivational aspects of autonomy. They have tried to prove that a control process which kills individual initiative defeats its own ends, as it frustrates the motivation of the controlled to really perform; and by asking for individual initiative one actually improves organisational performance (75, 77, 78). To a certain extent they have been successful. On the other hand, situations are known in which initiative killing controls work very well (7, 79). Also sometimes increased autonomy does not lead to higher motivation and performance (80, 81).

The relationship between individual autonomy and organisational performance is by no means a straightforward one. May be due to pseudo-autonomy. We feel that real autonomy comes only with the proper margin that can be manifested in releasing or recovering 'awareness', 'sponteneity' and 'intimacy' on the part of the players. The awareness will make players in the present and not elsewhere, past or the future. Spontaneity will provide them option, the freedom to choose 'ones' feelings from the assortment available. It means liberation, liberation from the compulsion to play games. This does not mean that players are not earnest while playing. They know they are playing and, therefore, they are fully involved and earnest.

Although play has a necessary element of spontaneity, but it is also concerned with order and form. Organised games have rules to which the players must adhere, and a game is spoiled if the rules are broken (67). In this way, a game is microcosm set apart from ordinary life, and much better ordered than our habitual, chaotic existence. The game displays a formalised pattern in which each player knows his task, and how he should behave. For the duration of the game, the participants have the delight of knowing exactly what is expected of them. Autonomy also develops intimacy, which means the spontaneous game-free candidness of an aware person. It has been established experimentally (64) that eidetical perception evokes affection, and that candidness mobilises positive feelings among players (64). This they do by encouraging the players to look at each other directly and to talk freely.

3.2.3 *CAN BUDGETING BE PLAYED AS A GAME*

The motivation through games and play is a remarkably neglected area, a blind spot in motivation theory, but an exception is a book by Fraser(76):

> 'We recognize...that sportsmanship is an admirable quality in a person and one which is linked up with emotional maturity, self-control and the ability to make a strong competitive effort while at the same time keeping it within the framework of a set of rules. In our games environments,....We have got the relation between the personal qualities of the individual and the working of the group pretty well sorted out. We might do well to transfer

some of our concepts of sportsmanship to other groupings in life also, and use them to interpret what is happening in our working life and our family life. In these groupings the roles have not been so well defined nor do the conventions seem always to have the same kind of authority. If we accepted a similar code of behaviour to that which governs our sports life in this country at the present day, many of our difficulties might be clarified' (p.195-196).

We find clues to it in the form of management games (82), business games (83), games of budget control (11) etc. During the interviews with budget managers and budgetees, several of them spontaneously expressed the budget system in game terms. One top financial executive commented, budget is a biggest game in the world, if you know how to play it'. Tovey(84) also quoted a British executive saying "What is a budget? It is a game-illegal but still a game". Recently in the U.S.A. Fuyunme(85) has defended the game approach for controllers in working with operating management:

'A metaphorical comparison can be made between the profit and loss statement and a baseball score sheet. Such a comparison can often jolt a manager into realising his deficiency in understanding the game of management. The psychology of 'game participation' is constructive, while the approach of control for control's sake engenders an attitude of being oppressed. It is important to gain the foreman's confidence as a participating player by illustrating that every action can materially effect profits. The point is, when supervision can think management terms and rules with the same facility and interest as their favourite game, then we have a management body that can begin to play the game as a team, with direction and purpose. The purpose is to make profits as there is no substitute for winning games' (p.52).

We may now consider how budgeting can be played as a game by the budgetees in the organisational setting. We have not introduced the concept of informal organisation initially as has been done by Sterdy (31), Argyris(7), McGregor(86) and Likert(87), but we have tried to introduce this concept in the formal setting of the organisation as is done by Hofstede(11). We have seen in the earlier paragraphs that budget will be self-destroying if it is adopted in the mechanistic way.

If we could introduce the 'margin' or 'scope' in the budget system, we may think of achieving desired results in the satisfaction of both budgetees and the organisation. This is the condition that makes it possible to exercise budget as a game.

The concept of budgetary slack has been suggested by Simon and March(88) to describe an original slack which is an unintended play in the budget system of an organisation. They have related this to inter-group conflict within the organisation. If the slack becomes less in the crisis periods, there will be more inter-group conflicts. When resources are restricted and this slack is taken up, the relations among individual members and sub-groups in the organisation become more nearly a strictly competitive game. The organisational slack has thus a connotation of wastefulness. The concept of play in our study on the other hand is a condition for reaching a psychological and economic optimism for avoiding the waste of destroying people's motivation.

Due to the incorporation of the 'play' element in 'game' conflict (70) may sometimes arise among two or more persons or units when the outcome does not maximise the pay off to everybody. But still there is an element of co-ordination; since there exists for atleast two of the players the possibility that they can do better by co-ordinating their resources than by acting alone. A coalition (89) can be formed to determine the joint use of resources and the outcome of the decision in a mixed motive situation involving more than two units.

For many groups, 'the rules of the game' strongly encourage the group of work jointly against a common antagonist such as the environment or outside world. It is greatly to the advantage of the five members of a basketball team, for instance, to avoid fragmentation into competing individuals of sub-groups.

But there is every possibility of resistance to introducing 'margin' or 'scope' in the budget system by the present business culture, because of both bureaucratic tradition and the Taylorist deterministic inheritance of the 'one best way' of doing. However, in our changing society, the inheritance is outdated. As one researcher (90) recently put it:

'My own researches showed that there is only 'one best way of doing most things' is closely linked with the inability to maintain effective performance in changing condition' (p.73).

In Chapter 4, we shall see how the experimental data support the theory that a budget system will have an optimal effect on motivation, when there is a sufficient margin in the system within which budget fulfilment can be seen as a 'sport' or 'game'. This means several things; it means a motivation from within not through pressure from outside goes with lower job satisfaction; motivation from within goes with higher job satisfaction. It also means that no energy will be split in fighting the system. Most people accept the basic fact that there are rules. Finally, if the game is well played that will provide co-operation. It is a social game in the sense that different departments in the organisation are fellow players, not antagonists. The antagonist is the outside world, real competitors on the market, impending cost increases etc. Games are the most thriliing when played against odds. The only part of the game where departments play against each other is the game of standard setting. Standards are often set by a game like bargaining between line and staff. We have shown in later chapters that this bargaining phase can be a positive contribution to the total game, provided that certain conditions are fulfilled.

Creating the game situation demands certain attitudes of higher management and specially of the immediate supervisor of the budgetees. This is really a crucial factor. Technical provisions in the budget system can help to develop the bargain spirit which is a condition for the game spirit.

3.3 RESEARCH FOUNDATIONS OF BUDGETING

The theoretical framework developed above in section 3.1 and 3.2 helps to highlight and formalize some psychological concepts that need to be considered. Of course, such formalism, however logical or elegant, are not enough in and of themselves to justify a theory. Hence an empirical foundation is desired or failing this, some kind of testing and validation is required. Apart from the study by Hofstede (11), others (refer page no.6, section 1.3) do not really deal with the problem of budgetees' responses to budget systems extensively used in organisations. There is no systematic accumulation of evidence where the desired empirical foundation can be readily secured.

Failing access to broad based and systematic studies on budgetees' behaviour under different budgetary arrangements, the following seems to be the best alternative sources of empirical information: (1) studies that have been made on workers' reactions to various control systems practised in organisations; and (2) psychological studies which are more or less germane to the topic of our interest. The choice of studies discussed below is based on the relevance of each work to the present study.

3.3.1 *ASPIRATION LEVELS*

It has been suggested that level of aspiration is a goal that, when barely achieved is associated with its subjective feeling of success; when not achieved it leads to a subjective feeling of failure (92). Evidence of the relationship between level of aspiration and performance is as under:

Bayton(93) while testing three hundred subject's performance on seven Arithmetic problems, found that a higher level of aspiration was followed by higher performance. Becker and Green(94) concluded from reviewing the literature that level of aspiration not only describes a goal for future attainment, but also it partially insures that an individual will expend a more than minimum amount of energy, if necessary, to perform at or above the level. Cook(95) concluded that the level of aspiration of participants was raised or lowered as a result of success or failure in performance. With this finding, Cook has also implied that success or failure are equally likely to produce changes in aspiration levels.

From an extensive review of literature, Child and Whitting(96) summarised their findings as follows:

- Success generally leads to a raising of the level of aspiration, failure to a lowering.
- The greater the success, greater is the probability of a rise in the level of aspiration; the greater the failure, greater is the

probability of a lowering.

- Shifts in the level of aspiration are in part a function of changes in the subject's confidence in his ability to attain goals.
- Failure is more likely than success to lead to withdrawal in the form of avoiding setting a level of aspiration.
- Effects of failure on level of aspiration are more varied than those of success.

Stedry(31) concluded that, other things being equal

- aspiration levels will move relative to the actual costs depending on the degree of discrepancy between actual costs and aspired costs is not greater than an amount known as the discouragement point. Aspiration would be set higher on the next period of performance measurement;
- a person will be discouraged if the discrepancy is greater than the discouragement point. In this case, aspirations would move downward; and
- if the discrepancy is greater than the failure point, the system would cease to exist or a new one would be needed. Otherwise, the individual concerned would resign.

3.3.2 *TIGHT OR LOOSE STANDARDS*

Lewin and Dembo etc.(92) concluded that subjects initially tend to set performance goals at higher levels than previous performance levels and then tend to keep them higher. However, if the subjects are unsuccessful in achieving goals, the levels of aspiration in the following periods are not as high as when the subjects are successful. The degree to which new goals are higher depends upon the degree of success attained in achieving previous goals. Fryer (97) found that forcing subjects to set goals, increase the level of performance most when the task was difficult. He also found that the process of goal setting had a greater effect on performance than did a knowledge of results.

Locke and Bryan(98), in a series of twelve studies found that the higher the intended level of achievement, the higher the level of performance. Stedry and Kay(99) found that when superiors considered very difficult goals impossible to attain instead of being challenging, their performance decreased significantly. Hofstede(11) stated that tight budget goals lead to higher motivation; beyond a certain limit, however, tightening of budget goals reduces motivation.

Locke and Bryan(98) found that specific goals resulted in significantly higher levels of performance than when subjects were merely told to do their best. Locke also found that with boring tasks, setting of goals increases interest. They found that subjects who were given more time to do a task took more time and set easier goals than subjects given the minimum amount of time necessary for goal success, according to their abilities. Locke and others have concluded that performance dissatisfaction depends on the relationship of actual performance to one's performance goals.

3.3.3 *PARTICIPATION IN BUDGET SETTING*

Davis(100) defines participation as the mental and emotional involvement of a person in a group situation which encourages him to contribute to group goals and share responsibility in them. Argyris (7) pointed out that goals are accepted if individual members are allowed to come together in a group, and take part in defining the steps by which these goals will be accomplished. Coch and French (75) found that people tend to support what they help to create. They also found that participation improves morale, much lower turnover rate, fewer grievances about piece rates, and less aggression against the supervisor.

French, Israel and Ass(81) in studying participation in a Norwegian factory found that workers' participation increases job satisfaction by satisfying important needs, such as the need to be valued and appreciated by others. Vroom(80) found that active participation seems to be desired by employees. It makes them feel more a part of the activities, less dominated by a superior, more independent, and thus, improves the employees' attitude towards his job. Hofstede(11) stated that in a budgeting system higher participation did lead to higher budget motivation although participation in the setting of technical, and non-financial standards had no correlation with budget motivation.

French, Key and Meyer(101) showed no significant difference in goal attainment between participative and non-participative groups. Steers(102) found positive and significant relationships between participation in task-goal-setting and job satisfaction and involvement, but no relationship between participation and employee performance.

Milani(103) found positive and significant correlation between participation in budget setting and attitudes towards the job and company, but the relationship between participation and job performance was very weak. Swieringa and Moncur(17) found higher need satisfaction among managers who were consulted on their budgets than those who were not consulted.

3.3.4 *LINE AND STAFF RELATIONSHIPS*

Status differences, or more accurately role conflict between line and staff personnel are an important source of dysfunctional consequences. Problems of conflict between line and staff affect the usefulness of budget motivation and participation. The basic difficulty arises because of differences in the way budget staff and line personnel understand the budget system and relate it to each other.

Simon(30) summarised his conclusions as under:

- It is essential for the controllers department to develop direct and active channels of communication with line management.
- Development of staff and facilities for special studies is more important than elaboration of periodic accounting reports.
- Within the controller's department it is advisable to separate personnel into (a) book-keeping and reports publishing, (b) assistance to the line in current analysis of accounting information, and (c) special studies in project terms together with line and staff people.
- It is relatively unimportant whether the plant controller reports to the plant manager or to the company controller, as long as he has the authority to provide reports to the plant management as requested.
- There should be a plan for the development of accounting personnel in human relations.

Argyris(7) also reported the reasons of conflict between line and staff as under:

- Budget staff viewed their role as essentially one of criticism. They considered themselves to be 'watchdog' whose principal function was to be constantly looking for deviations to report to top management.
- The accountants believed that budgets were a legitimate means of applying pressure on line employees.
- They saw the budget as a challenge which they had provided to the production people and were at a loss to explain why line personnel failed to appreciate being challenged in this manner.
- The reports included only results and not reasons for the results.
- Accountants were considered inflexible, they are reluctant to change their standard as conditions change.
- Budgets were not realistic.
- Budget staff was never satisfied and was constantly applying pressure for ever increasing goals. The line employee resented such pressure, since it implied that they lacked an adequate interest in their jobs and would lose their motivation if it were not for the budget.

3.3.5 *SUPERIOR-SUBORDINATE RELATIONSHIP*

Davis(100) concluded that 'employee-oriented' supervisors tend to get better productivity, motivation and worker satisfaction. Likert (104) asserts that the supervisor who obtains the highest productivity is one who is 'supportive, friendly and helpful rather than hostile and endeavours to treat people in a sensitive, considerate way.' Kahn, Maccoby and Morse(105) indicated that highly productive supervisors were typically characterised as employee-oriented for they tended to describe as most important the human relations aspects in their jobs. On the other hand, those in charge of low productivity work groups were typically characterised as 'production-centered' for they tended to consider their subordinates primarily as 'people to get the work done'.

Katz, Maccoby, Gurin and Floor(106) found that men in high

productivity groups more frequently described as their supervisors as taking a personal interest in them, helpful in training them for better jobs and as being less punitive than men in low productivity sections. Likert(104) found that managers who have a supportive attitude toward their men and endeavour to build them into well knit teams obtain appreciably higher productivity than managers who have a threatening attitude.

White and Lippitt(105) in their study of boys club found that the democratic group was more productive, possessed stronger work motivations, performed more original work and had a high degree of group-mindedness than the autocratic or laissez-faire groups. Kahn and Katz(108) found that the high producing supervisors were more 'employee-oriented' than their low-producing colleagues. The low productivity supervisors emphasized production and technical aspects of the job, and tended to think of their employees as people to get the work done. The high producing supervisors were predominantly employee-identified, according to their own report. The low productivity supervisors were, for the most part, management-identified.

Hartmann and Newcomb(109) showed that following seven out of twelve items have been ranked by 1,00,000 employees stating the importance of good supervision in producing job satisfaction:

1. Receiving help necessary to get results expected by management.
2. Being able to find out whether work is improving.
3. Reasonable certainty of being able to get fair hearing and square deal in case of grievances.
4. Encouragement to seek advice in case of real problem.
5. Being given reasons for changes which are ordered in work.
6. Not getting contradictory or conflicting orders.
7. Being given to understand completely the results which are expected in a job.

3.3.6 *EVALUATION OF PERFORMANCE AND FEEDBACK OF RESULTS*

Colenan(110) reported that evaluation of performance can be

made effective provided: (a) superior and subordinate jointly reach agreement on critical elements of the subordinate's job; (b) superior and subordinate jointly decide on ways performance will be measured; (c) superior and subordinate jointly develop short-term targets; (d) main emphasis is placed on superior-subordinate counselling using objective data whenever possible; and (e) appraisal focuses on the results achieved by the subordinate rather than on his personal characteristics.

Ammons(111) concluded that: (a) knowledge of performance affects rate of learning and level reached by learning; (b) knowledge of performance affects motivation, the most common effects of knowledge of performance is to increase motivation; (c) the more specific the knowledge of performance, the more rapid is improvement and higher the level of performance; (d) the longer the delay in giving knowledge of performance, the less effect the given performance has; and (e) when knowledge of performance is decreased, performance drops.

Pryer and Bass(112) found that the groups receiving feedback solved their problems more accurately and became more highly motivated to solve future problems than the group that was not getting the feedback. Zajonc(113) reported that feedback about both - individual performance and the performance of the group as a whole - increase the performance of individual members. Smith and Knight (114) reported that personnel feedback of one member to another was to improve the efficiency of all. Weitz, Antoinette and Wallace (115) found that those who received periodic production bulletins and personal letters communicating their performance improved the average performance of a group of agents receiving no feedback actually decreased as compared to a base period.

Miller(116) found that increasing the amount of feedback from foreman to workers improved the latters' performance. Hundal(117) found that groups of industrial workers who received feedback had higher output than workers who did not. He also found that the more specific, relevant and timely the feedback, the greater the positive effects on performance. French(118) also reported that feedback was most effective when it was directly relevant to the task.

Leavitt and Mueller(119) in a study of the effects of varying amount of feedback, found that performance improved as the quality of feedback improved. They also observed that the absence of any feedback was accompanied by high hostility and low confidence. On the other hand, a high level of feedback was accompanied by friendly attitudes and high confidence.

Hamblin and Wiggins(120) found that as ambiguity decreased with better information, innovative behaviour increased and ritualism decreased. Smith(121) found that as role expectations became clearer, group satisfaction and effectiveness increased. Kay, Meyer and French(122) found that under certain conditions in which the appraisee expected favourable feedback, critical appraisal had a negative effect on attitudes.

Locke and Bryan(98) in two studies found that feedback did not improve performance and that goal setting itself contributed more to performance than knowledge of results. In another study they found that feedback did improve performance when the subjects used it to establish goals. Locke seems to feel that the feedback is used as a means of comparing performance with some previously established goal or standard. Similarly, research by Dorris M. Cook(95) using college students in an experiment on budgeting, indicated that the interest and satisfaction of the participants was directly related to the frequency of feedback.

3.3.7 *ORGANISATION CHARACTERISTICS*

Many studies (123, 124, 125, 126) have reported that budget oriented behaviour is bound to be contingent upon environment and organisation characteristics such as size, market, complexity of activities, technology, autonomy and the degree to which activities are structured.

Worthy(127) revealed that organisation-size alone unquestionably is one of the most important factors in determining the quality of employee relationships: the smaller the size of the unit, the higher the morale of the employees and vice-versa. Marriott(128) also reported that the size factor affects productivity directly. Significant (though low) correlations were found between output and size and smaller work groups showed consistently larger output in each factory. Worthy himself suggested that the overcomplexity of organisation structure is one of the most important and fundamental causes of poor management.

Whitin (129) reported that centralisation and large size make perception of the worker's needs difficult, communication between the decision makers and those who carry out their decisions becomes complicated and are subject to more interference (noince). Chaplin and Tsouderous(130) revealed that ordinary members become more passive and dissociated from the central purposes of the organisation and leadership becomes further removed from the plan. The choice between decentralisation with structuring and centralisation is limited to some extent by internal and external conditions faced by the organisation. Several studies (131, 132) have shown that the size of the organisation is positively associated with structuring of activities and negatively associated with centralisation.

Technological sophistication is also positively associated with structuring of activities (132). It tied to technology and means for standardised mass production, they formalise role definitions and decentralise decision-making authority (133). Concurrently, these organisations develop means for maintaining control by utilising procedures for defining and measuring role performance.

3.3.8 *DEMOGRAPHIC VARIABLES*

A few studies have been devoted to the input into budget system which originating from the kind of people the budgetees are themselves: how old they are, how long they have been in their jobs, what is the influence of their hierarchical and educational level and which aspects of their personalities and their cultural norms play a role in the system.

A study of woman office workers by the U.S. Department of Labour (134) showed no essential difference in output over the ages ranging from under 25 to 65 and above. The younger women were even slightly below the levels achieved by the older women. In a study of sales activity, Maher(135) obtained the relationship between age and performance on a large sample of salesman. The performance of older salesman turned out to be better than that of the young ones. Further evidence of the absence of significant differences in work performance at various ages comes from a study of Bowers(136) where for traits such as accuracy, initiative, job knowledge, tactfulness and co-operativeness, there was no difference between age groupings from 18 to over 60. Older workers were considered slower but not much so. They were rated higher on steadiness and conscientiousness.

Brighter office workers have been reported as being slightly more dissatisfied with their jobs (137). Intelligent factory workers in England were found to be more dissatisfied with repetitive work (138). On the other hand, some studies reported no relationship between job satisfaction and intelligence (139) and education (140). Still more extreme, one nationwide survey of factory workers revealed that workers who did not get beyond high school felt somewhat more strongly than those who went to college that their work was too simple (141). Taking workers as a whole, it seems that intelligence and education are only minor factors in determining job satisfaction. In job rotation on restrictive tasks may not only serve to reduce the feeling of boredom (142, 143, 144, 145) but simultaneously raise the status of the worker in his own eyes, in those of his fellow workers, associates and community. A prime effect of the opportunity to participate in decision-making may well be to raise the status of the worker as he sees it and as it is viewed by other people in the plant. The worker, as do people in other situations, wants to be in the role of an 'important person'. He seeks to enjoy this feeling of worth, the recognition and respect of others as has been suggested by Burns(146).

The findings of Gurin, Verroff and Felds(147) on job level and job satisfaction showed substantial differences between the level of satisfaction reported by persons in different occupational categories, 42% of persons employed in professional-technical occupations reported that they were very satisfied with their jobs as compared with only 13% of workers in the unskilled category. In general, reported job satisfaction declined with occupational level. However, that relatively low level of satisfaction was reported by clerical and sales workers should be noted. Only 61% of clerical and 68% of sales persons state that they were very satisfied with their jobs as compared with 80%, 76% and 75% of farmers, skilled and semi-skilled workers, respectively.

Herzberg, Mausuer, Peterson and Capwell(148) summarize the results with the following descriptions of satisfied and dissatisfied workers: the satisfied worker is, in general, a more flexible, better adjusted person who has come from a superior family environment, or who has the capacity to overcome the effects of an inferior environment. He is realistic about his own situation and about his job; in contrast, the dissatisfied worker is often rigid, inflexible, unrealistic in his choice of goals, unable to overcome environmental obstacles, generally unhappy and dissatisfied.

Whenever a person acts in accordance with the expectations of others, his behaviour is social. A person grows to manhood in a culture, which is his man-made environment of beliefs, customs, knowledge and practices. Culture is the conventionalised behaviour of his society, and it influences all his actions; therefore, any understanding of an employee's behaviour must be preceded by study and understanding of the culture in which he lives.

SUMMARY OF THE SURVEYS

The studies presented above provide a cross section of evidence available about human behaviour which might be applicable to an individual in a budget-controlled activity. More of course, could be presented, but it is hoped that this brief survey will at least provide some background for the analysis and experiments which will be dealt within the following chapter.

To summarise, there is evidence that individuals form either individual goals or estimates of their performance (or perhaps both). On the other hand, it is not precisely clear which of these are being formed at any given instant. The motivating effect of budgets becomes stronger when they become tighter, but who has set the standards is the crucial question. Studies also showed that active participation in planning by those responsible for performance helps to promote understanding and acceptance of the plans, clarifies responsibilities for performance and induces better relations between line and staff personnel, but participation is not panacea for all problems all the time to achieve ultimate satisfaction. The adoption of overall goals of the organisation by the participants as their own goals, reduces conflict, improves communication and minimizes the adverse effects of department-centeredness. During performance evaluation and feedback sessions, the superior's role is a crucial element in the subordinate's future motivations. Demographic variables of the participants and organisation characteristics also play key role but not a decisive one in employee's performance and job satisfaction.

Field studies have shown conflicting results and only isolated examples indicate the possibility of introducing an adequate budget system. A further weakness from the stand-point of this study is that almost all studies in this area have been directed primarily towards the behaviour of production workers, as distinct from budgetees and budget managers.

Bearing these kinds of considerations and qualifications in mind, the gist of the experiment actually undertaken is described in Chapter 4.

4

INPUT AND OUTPUT OF BUDGET SYSTEM

The purpose of this chapter is to empirically verify the input-output variables of budget system on the basis of opinion of budget managers and budgetees. The analysis is divided into three sections. Section 4.1 contains the output variables of budget system selected in this study. This is followed by section 4.2 which is devoted to the identification of inputs of budget system that makes budget standards relevant to the budgetees' task from low to high and attitude of budgetees from negative to positive. Finally, section 4.3 summarises the data relating to the justification of using budgeting as a game rather than a tool of accounting control.

4.1 OUTPUT VARIABLES OF BUDGET SYSTEM

Profitability (measured in terms of job performance) and well-being of all employees (measured in terms of job satisfaction) have been taken as the output variables of budget system in this study. These are described as under:

4.1.1 *PROFITABILITY*

Normally, profitability is measured in terms of profits by most of the companies. It is also reflected in the under mentioned opinion expressed by the respondents while responding to our questionnaire:

"We are not in business to make steel,
we are not in business to build ships,

we are not in business to erect buildings,
we are in business to make money."

This states the fundamental fact with admirable directness. However, profit as a criterion of measuring profitability has its own limitations. Measurement of profit in itself is influenced by many factors other than those which are being appraised. Moreover, since it is a measure of end-results, it may be a delayed indicator of organisational health. Profit may be high or low as a result of many conditions other than the quality of organisation. Cyclical swings in business are beyond the control of management and may sharply restrict or expand current profits. High levels of profits may appear long after an organisation has begun 'coasting', i.e., benefiting from earlier but presently reduced effectiveness.

Keeping in view the limitations of profit as a criterion of measuring profitability, i.e., the effectiveness of individual and group performance, it is measured in terms of individual performance of budgetees. Four variables - 'budget influences budgetee's performance', 'budget stimulates budgetees for better performance', 'possible to work better at reduced costs through budgets' and 'instructions, not budgets will improve future performance' - have been selected to measure the performance of budgetees. These variables have been selected on the basis of evidence of their effectiveness as the criteria of measuring job performance in earlier studies (11, 18, 21 and 22). The opinion of budget managers and budgetees about these variables as the criteria of measuring performance and hence profitability is summarised below in Table 4.1.

TABLE 4.1 **Budget Managers and Budgetees' Opinion about the Variables of Job Performance under Budgetary Conditions (Figures in %)**

Performance Variables	Response									
	Always		Mostly		Sometimes		Seldom		Never	
	BM	OM	BM	OM	BM	OM	BM	OM	BM	OM
Influences	75	46	12	26	09	11	02	16	02	01
Stimulates	41	31	30	43	18	24	06	01	05	01
Better Work at reduced costs	31	32	33	34	29	23	05	10	02	01
Instructions, not budgets	79	03	05	05	08	14	02	43	06	35

N.B.: B.M. = Budget Managers; O.M. = Operating Managers (budgetees)

Table 4.1 reveals clearly that budgetees are not favourably inclined to work with (3%), but they are of the opinion that budgets not only influence their productivity (46%) but also stimulate them for better performance (31%). They are also of the opinion that it is possible to work better at reduced costs through budgets (32%) because they get stimulus out of this system and little dictation on the job to be done (97%). Even after this high opinion towards job performance through budget system their lack of enthusiasm to work with budgets can be an indication of certain reservations to the present system of budgeting practised in their respective organisations.

Table 4.1 also gives more or less the same impression of budget managers except their preference to the budget system (75%) as a tool to influence productivity of budgetees. They have a strong opinion indicating their preference (79%) to work with budgets. This may be because of differences with budgetees in terms of educational and cultural background. Regarding the other variables of job performance also budget managers give the better impression of their attitude towards budget system as compared to budgetees.

In Table 4.1, variable - 'instructions, not budgets will improve future performance'- gives a clear-cut point of departure between budgetees and the budget managers in adopting and praticising the budget system in the organisations. Why this departure is there and how to fill this gap is the major issue that will be found to some extent with the help of inputs suggested by budget managers as well as budgetees in the following chapters.

The consistency and homogeneity of opinion of budgetees and budget managers about job performance variables under budgetary conditions is presented below in Table 4.2.

TABLE 4.2 **Mean, Standard Deviation and Coefficient of Variation of the Variables given in Table 4.1**

Performance Variables	Mean		S.D.		C.V.	
	BM	OM	BM	OM	BM	OM
Influences	1.57	1.90	.82	.90	52	47
Stimulates	2.05	1.56	1.15	.66	56	42
Better work at reduced costs	2.20	2.44	1.02	1.04	46	43

Instructions, not budgets	2.31	3.99	1.10	1.02	48	26

NB: C.V. = Coefficient of Variation.

Table 4.2 indicates the lack of consistency and homogeneity in budget manager's opinion. Budgetees are more consistent in their responses as compared to budget managers. Wide dispersion among responses justifies consideration of all the variables of job performance rather than a composite index of these in the measurement of individual as well as group performance.

The interdependence of these variables is summarised below in Table 4.3 in order to further verify the above proposition.

TABLE 4.3 **Intercorrelations among the Performance Variables**

	Performance Variables			
Performance Variables	Influences productivity	Stimulates performance	Work better at reduced costs	Instructions, not budgets
Influences	-	.072	.036	-.068
Stimulates	(.335)*	-	.094	.070
Work better at reduced costs	(-.210)***	(-.303)*	-	.053
Instructions, not budgets	(.173)	(-.128)	(-.036)	-

NB: *<.01 level of significance; ***<.05 level of significance. Figures given in parentheses pertains to B.M.

Table 4.3 reveals that all the variables are least correlated with each other in the opinion of budgetees. It means that they are independent and complementary to each other and hence the contribution of each variable towards the measurement of performance will be additional.

However, in the case of budget managers, the job performance variable - 'budget stimulates budgetees for better performance'- is significantly correlated with the another variables of job performance- 'budgets influence budgetee's performance', and 'It is possible to work better at reduced costs through budgets'- at .01 level of significance. This indicates that if budgetees work through budgets, it stimulates them for better performance and also influences their productivity. Except the variable - 'instructions, not budgets will improve budgetee's performance', all other variables are significantly correlated in the case of budget managers.

This wide gap between the opinion of budget managers and budgetees about the output variables of budget system gives rise to the question of finding out the solution in the form of inputs of budget system.

4.1.2 *WELL-BEING OF EMPLOYEES*

Well-being is defined as a good or satisfactory condition of existence; or a state characterised by health, happiness and prosperity. The term well-being is broader than simply job satisfaction and morale, but they are used interchangeably. Job satisfaction is sometimes measured by turnover and absenteeism of the employees, but they are not perfect measures of well-being of the employees. Keeping in view the limitation, job satisfaction is measured in terms of four variables. These are: 'budgetees like the department where they work', 'budgetees feel agitated and nervous', 'budgetees enjoy their job' and 'budgetees feel under pressure'. These variables are selected on the basis of their frequency of appearance as important variables of measuring job satisfaction in the earlier studies (11, 23, 24). The opinion of budget managers and budgetees about these variables of measuring job satisfaction is summarised below in Table 4.4.

TABLE 4.4 **Opinion of Budget Managers and Budgetees about the Job Satisfaction Variables**

(Figures in %)

Job Satisfaction Variables	Always		Mostly		Response Sometimes		Seldom		Never	
	BM	OM	BM	OM	BM	OM	BM	OM	BM	OM
Like	47	46	37	37	11	15	00	00	01	01
Agitate	03	11	07	07	16	14	40	29	34	49
Enjoy	52	51	38	36	06	12	03	01	01	01
Pressure	06	11	16	11	28	45	31	22	19	11

Table 4.4 clearly indicates that budgetees like their departments (46%) and enjoy their assignments (51%) on account of less pressure (11%) and non-irritable attitude (11%) of top management towards budgetees. Budget managers also corroborate the above opinion of budgetees and state that budgetees like (47%) their departments and enjoy (52%) their jobs when they feel less pressure (6%) and non-irritable (3%) attitude from the top.

The consistency and homogeneity of the opinion of budget managers and budgetees is presented below in Table 4.5.

TABLE 4.5 **Mean, Standard Deviation and Coefficient of Variation of the Responses given in Table 4.4**

Job Satisfaction Variables	Mean		S.D.		C.V.	
	BM	OM	BM	OM	BM	OM
Like	1.70	1.74	.72	.85	42	50
Agitate	4.14	3.94	1.04	1.01	25	26
Enjoy	1.64	1.64	.74	.81	45	49
Pressure	3.10	3.41	1.13	1.17	36	34

Table 4.5 reveals that the opinion of budgetees and budget managers about the variables of job satisfaction are more or less consistent.

The interdependence of the job satisfaction variables in the budget system is summarised below in Table 4.6.

TABLE 4.6 **Intercorrelations among the Job Satisfaction Variables**

Job Satisfaction Variables	Job Satisfaction Variables			
	Like	Agitate	Enjoy	Pressure
Like	-	(-.227)*	(.246)*	-.076
Agitate	(-.274)*	-	.003	.230*
Enjoy	(.653)*	(-.379)*	-	.092
Pressure	(-.140)	(.199)	(-.105)	-

N.B.: * < .01 level of significance.
Figures given in parentheses pertain to budget managers.

Table 4.6 reveals that the variables, 'budgetees like the department where they work' and 'superiors make budgetees agitated and nervous' are significantly correlated with the variables, 'budgetees enjoy their job' and 'budgetees feel under pressure on their jobs' at .01 level of significance respectively. The highly significant correlation among these variables is not only reflected in low turnover and absenteeism but also in their liking the departments and enjoying the jobs. Their liking and enjoyment also depend upon non-irritable attitude of top management and exercising of lesser pressure upon budgetees.

Table 4.6 further indicates that budget managers' opinions have a similar pattern of correlations. The variable, 'budgetees like the department where they work' is significantly correlated with the variables, 'budgetees enjoy their jobs' and 'superiors make budgetees less agitated and nervous' - at .01 level of significance. It clearly brings out that well-being of employees depends upon the non-irritable and pressure -free atmosphere of the organisations.

4.1.3 *JOB PERFORMANCE AND JOB SATISFACTION*

The opinion of budget managers and budgetees about the relationships between job satisfaction and job performance is summarised below in Table 4.7.

TABLE 4.7 **Intercorrelations among the Job Satisfaction and Job Performance**

Performance	Job Satisfaction Variables			
Variables	Like	Agitate	Enjoy	Pressure
Influences productivity	.045 (.325)*	-.054 (-.392)*	.070 (.291)*	-.020 (-.154)
Stimulates Performance	.055 (.219)***	-.013 (-.241)**	.085 (.280)*	.013 .(-.220)***
Better work at reduced costs	.055 (.038)	-.014 (.012)	.082 (.220)***	.-049 -.240**
Instructions not budgets	.084 (.052)	-.079 (.124)	.065 (.011)	-.039 (-.076)

N.B. * <.01 ** < .02 *** < .05

Figures given in parentheses pertain to budget managers.

Table 4.7 reveals that in the opinion of budgetees none of the variables of job satisfaction is significantly correlated with the variables of job performance even at .05 level of significance. It means that all the variables of job performance and job satisfaction are independent and least correlated with each other and hence relevant to our study.

The budget managers' view-point is little different. They are of the opinion that if budgetees like their department, enjoy their job and are free from irritated attitude of top management, the performance of budgetees will improve. Analysis of data further reveals that pressure-free atmosphere of organisation stimulates budgetees for better performance. One may thus conclude that irritating attitude of top management towards their subordinates have the maximum negative effect over the performance of budgetees. Enjoyment of the job is considered by the budget managers as the best formula for improving job performance of budgetees. Table 4.7 clearly shows the relevance and appropriateness of all the variables of job satisfaction and job performance to judge the profitability in the interest of shareholders and well-being of employees of all ranks.

4.2 INPUT OF BUDGET SYSTEM

The rotated factor loadings of 46 variables for budgetees' budget-oriented behaviour items are summarized below in Table 4.8. Table 4.8 also presents the correlations of budget-oriented behaviour variables with 'playing budgeting as a game' and 'using budgeting as a tool of accounting control'.

The rotated factor loadings of 47 variables for budget manager's budget-oriented behaviour items are summarized below in Table 4.9 It also presents the correlationships of budget-oriented behaviour variables with 'playing budgeting as a game', and 'using budgeting as a tool of accounting control'.

TABLE 4.8 Factor Loadings of Budget Oriented Behaviour Questions of Budgetees and Their Relationship with Budget Systems

S.N.	Variable's Name	Rotated Factor Loadings						Budget System	
		Factor I	Factor II	Factor III	Factor IV	Factor V	Factor VI	Accounting Tool	Game to Play
1.	Superiors reject my ideas for improvements	.016	-.071	-.755*	-.026	-.000	.077	.000	-.044
2.	In this plant, my private interests are taken into account as much as possible	.805*	072	.034	.092	-.035	-.029	-.103	-.108
3.	The management information reports I get are sufficiently understandable	-.052	031	.035	-.036	-.065	.770*	-.015	-.089
4.	Budgets are set here without taking sufficient account of my problems	.178	-.562	-.010	.017	-.130	.003	.095	-.021
5.	If I am absent for a week, my department still keeps running well	.019	229	.086	-.007	.074	.210	.068	.005
6.	Staff take no interest in the goal-setting programme of my department	-.085	012	.039	-.792*	-.002	.034	.043	-.046
7.	I think my performance is justly appraised here on my ability to attain budget standards	.108	052	.299	.016	-.568*	-.088	-.010	-.046
8.	This plant is well managed	.003	020	-.010	.128	-.059	.009	.135	.185
9.	Supervisors ask my opinion about matters concerning my areas of work.	-.151	386	-.051	.203	.111	-.149	.021	.261#
10.	Supervisors are working continuously on cost reduction	-.022	-.022	-.700*	-.147	.080	.053	.079	.127

11. The people from budget department have a lack of understanding of my problems	.348	.043	-.182	-.475*	.118	-.118	.040	-.055
12. My seniors listen to my suggestions and complaints with an attitude of fair consideration	-.032	.039	.800	.099	.118	.143	.173	.047
13. The co-operation between the line and staff leaves much to be desired	.127	-.138	.040	-.481*	.046	.339	.072	.046
14. My career opportunities here depend first of all on myself	-.080	-.155	.74[illegible]	-.054	.057	-.102	-.093	-.106
15. Taking everything into account my department runs efficiently enough	.097	.075	-.035	-.124	.061	-.080	.105	.199
16. My superiors hold me personally accountable for budget variances in my department	-.328	.076	-.061	-.001	-.424*	.113	.053	.169
17. Budgeting helps me in knowing exactly which costs I am responsible for	.590*	-.123	.045	-.353	.046	.039	.041	.197
18. Superiors take personal interest in the budgetary problems of my department	-.140	.033	.837*	.077	-.060	.117	.082	-.010
19. I attend meetings of top management where budget variances are discussed	-.024	-.010	-.060	-.117	-.737*	.013	-.009	-.189
20. The budget is primarily developed to meet my department's interest first	.010	.802*	.064	.163	.002	-.072	-.084	.028

21. I think my budget goals are ambiguous and not very clear	.341	-.012	.096	.341	-.149	.218	.037	.042
22. I exercise maximum degree of influence in the determination of my budget goals	-.086	.754*	.030	-.015	.022	.115	.108	.006
23. I receive considerable amount of information about my budget achievements	.069	.051	-.081	.002	-.076	.730*	-.074	.018
24. I prefer the standards that can be easily attainable	.569*	.083	.170	.037	.166	.167	-.099	-.015
25. My superiors accept my budgets without reservations	-.030	.762*	.069	.115	-.079	-.017	.026	.035
26. I have really little voice in the formation of my budget goals	-.007	-.499*	-.102	-.133	.133	-.737	-.017	.110
27. Budget reports appraising performance are shown to me without delay	-.044	.061	.014	-.298	.303	-.362	-.025	.106
28. My budget goals are quite difficult to attain	-.410*	-.052	.000	-.009	-.090	-.018	.114	.106
29. I have complete autonomy in making decisions relating to my department's budgets	-.209	-.412*	-.368	.086	.350	-.108	-.028	-.057
30. I understand fully which of my budget goals are more important than others	-.453*	.030	-.131	.247	.148	.239	.132	-.054

31. My budget is not finalised until I am satisfied with it	.001	.687*	-.096	.052	-.032	-.135	.118	.237#
32. My superiors tell me about how well I am doing in terms of achieving my budget goals	.022	-.129	-.111	.290	-.145	-.415*	.088	.098
33. My budget goals require a great deal of efforts from me to achieve them	-.809*	-.208	.135	-.088	.161	.023	.133	.005
34. Budgeting requires high degree of skill and know-how on my part to attain them	-.529*	.068	-.237	.114	.036	.015	.092	-.079
35. I get instructions from different people working above me on budget matters	-.502*	-.007	-.006	-.397	-.105	.306	.118	.106
36. The setting of my budget goal is pretty much under my control	.135	-.412*	.050	.004	-.013	.122	-.149	.015
37. Assistance from staff department is available on budget matters with little persuation	-.064	.004	-.129	.813*	.013	-.022	.129	.052
38. Superiors tend to tell and demand in preference to ask or persuade on budget matters	-.061	.090	-.367	.086	-.050	.306	.018	-.017
39. Budget evaluation does not concern with human considerations	-.056	-.120	.014	-.097	-.759*	.075	.035	.012

40. I have complete control over the means of reaching my budget targets	-.083	-.046	-.041	.720*	-.138	-.111	.070	.164
41. I discuss budget items with staff whenever problem occurs without hesitation	-.083	-.046	-.041	.720*	-.138	-.111	.070	.164
42. My superiors join us in developing department's goals and priorities	.103	.102	.725*	-.067	.086	-.037	-.037	.018
43. My superiors are never satisfied with my explanation of budget variances in my department	.043	-.065	-.016	.235	-.588*	-.197	.096	-.031
44. Staff advice is very useful in achieving budget standards	-.158	.080	-.042	.635*	.071	.152	.096	.303#
45. Superiors enjoy free and frank dialogue with subordinates on budget matters	-.136	.052	-.221	.087	.143	.356	-.002	.104
46. Superiors encourage free flow of information and ideas among group members on budget matters	-.013	.020	.009	-.025	.046	-.824*	.063	-.078
Total contribution of each factor	17.60%	12.10%	10.50%	10.00%	9.40%	9.00%		

N.B. * Variables having factor loadings .40 or above. # < .01

TABLE 4.9 **Rotated Factor Loadings of Budget-Oriented Behaviour Questions of Budget Managers and Their Relationship with Budget System**

S.N.	Variable's Name	Rotated Factor Loadings						Budget System	
		I	II	III	IV	V	VI	Accounting Tool	Game to Play
1.	The line managers are ignorant about the job done by my department	.113	.021	.050	.813*	.076	.100	-.116	-.127
2.	In this organisation, private interests of budgetees are taken account of as much as possible	.716*	.036	-.019	-.289	-.088	.011	-.033	.039
3.	Staff department should leave more to the line	-.022	-.182	-.110	.811*	-.127	.079	-.195	.004
4.	The line managers are insufficiently cost-conscious	.058	.148	.073	-.824*	-.017	-.085	-.038	.021
5.	The directives from Head Office are limited to necessary minimum	-.046	.394	-.286	.194	.135	.117	.184	-.288#
6.	The first task of my department is service to management	-.299	.017	-.071	-.753*	-.133	.013	.241	.191
7.	The co-operation between line and staff department is smooth	-.049	-.014	-.013	-.859*	-.103	.008	.236	-.031
8.	Performance of managers is justly appraised here on their ability to attain budget standards	-.305	.160	.159	.260	.351	.079	.286#	-.103

9. This organisation is well managed	-.081	-.023	.379	-.023	-.086	- 217	.111	-.152
10. Superiors ask budgetees, opinion about matters concerning their areas of work	-.119	.528*	-.332	.227	.004	-.128	-.245	.236
11. A main task of budget variance report is to show superiors where their subordinates have failed	-.128	-.194	.022	-.257	.057	-.477*	.215	.106
12. Line management is sufficiently conscious of the need for reliable clerical data	-.606*	-.055	.171	-.098	.138	.110	.090	.022
13. Line management is well concerned of the importance of meeting quality standards	.017	-.145	-.044	-.532*	.088	-.032	.313#	.034
14. More co-operation is desired between my department and the line managers	-.236	.051	-.049	.577*	.215	.001	-.031	.20
15. Career opportunities of budgetees here depend first of all on themselves	-.025	-.088	-.402*	.310	.060	-.116	.026	.00
16. My department is insufficiently consulted in organisational problems	.127	-.520*	-.087	.129	-.229	.228	-.217	.047
17. The line managers do not spend enough efforts to meet production schedules	-.208	-.095	-.105	.694*	-010	-.033	-.005	-.414#
18. Line managers follow our advice	.106	-.350	-.211	-.441*	-.198	-.093	.042	.056
19. Reporting of budget information follows closely upon the acions	-.006	.081	- 211	-.004	-.194	-.837*	.096	-.178

20. Most managers feel a real sense of accomplishment when they meet their budgets	-.064	-.210	.052	-.423*	-.354	-.227	-.073	.294#
21. Reporting of budget information is limited to behaviours controllable by the budgetees	.051	-.315	-.116	.031	.019	.409*	.059	.022
22. Budgets are yardsticks used to evaluate performance	-.124	.050	.017	.096	.812*	-.122	.061	.055
23. Superiors encourage the line to use staff effectively	-.031	-.050	-.677*	-.063	.089	-.111	.318#	.081
24. Superiors recognise that time and efforts spent in training and educating managers by staff is an excellent investment	-.084	-.051	-.724*	.139	.239	.223	.328#	-.125
25. Superiors appreciate the suggestions regarding improvement in the process techniques of the organisation	-.151	-.198	-.642*	.188	-.102	-.154	.260	.168
26. Superiors hesitate in taking staff co-operation on budget matters	.100	-.015	.792*	-.047	.170	.119	.168	-.094
27. Budgeting tends to make budgetees feel dependent on superiors	-.165	.818*	.054	.038	-.116	-.035	.123	.203
28. Budgeting gives too much power to budget department	-.393	.557*	-.309	.087	.083	-.177	.153	.197
29. Budgeting forces line managers to bargain with the budget department	-.084	.644*	-.100	.071	.127	.119	-.024	-.254#
30. Budgeting tends to take away the freedom of the line managers	.237	-.446*	-.111	.175	.003	-.022	-.025	-.286#

31. Reporting of budget information is within the receivers responsibility	-.280	-.029	-.017	-.146	-.055	.744*	.189	-.180
32. Feed back is limited to areas where adequate performance measurement is possible	-.068	.064	-.128	.032	.009	.853*	.260#	-.032
33. Receivers of budget information participate in the feedback process	.003	-.379	.014	-.093	-.098	.404*	-.081	.192
34. Budgeting helps line in knowing exactly which costs they are responsible for	-.679*	-.106	.251	.134	-.055	-.213	.155	-.108
35. I think our budget goals are quite clear and accurate	.555*	-.137	046	-.139	-.338	.021	.171	.356#
36. Budgetees prefer the budgets that can be easily achieved	-.788*	.171	- 101	.037	-.013	.021	.210	-.090
37. Our budget requires a great deal of efforts from line to attain them	.615*	.132	.029	.084	.043	.249	.396#	.059
38. Budgeting requires high degree of skill and know-how on line manager's part to attain them	.425*	.123	.346	-.081	-.072	.012	.188	.302#
39. Line managers have absolute control over means of reaching their department's budgets	-.771*	-.066	-.012	-.045	-.079	-.006	.167	.308#
40. Budgets are not finalised till budgetees are satisfied	.042	-.677*	.284	.153	.185	.084	.092	.313#
41. I allow high degree of influence in the determination of budget standards to those who have to attain budgets	-.041	-.689*	.109	.095	.139	.013	.244	-.109

42. Budgetees have favourable attitudes towards participation	-.169	-.492*	.151	-.250	-.045	-.115	.033	.011
43. Line managers are personally held accountable for budget variances in their department	.101	.170	.052	-.240	-.459*	-.063	.346#	.090
44. Staff express their dissatisfaction when line managers show negative variances	-.249	-.061	.246	-.024	-.381	-.261	.154	.136
45. Budget variances are concerned only with physical targets	.071	.173	-.204	-.032	-.608*	.113	.974	.055
46. Line managers attend meetings where budget variances are discussed	.075	.002	-.058	-.111	-.867*	.080	.022	.107
47. Budget variances are considered as factors in the raising of line manager's pay	-.189	.041	-.065	.015	.849*	-.047	.194	.143
Total Contribution of each factor	18.7%	15.3%	11.8%	11.5%	10.7%	7.6%		

N.B. * Variables having factor loadings .40 and above. # <.01

Tables 4.8 and 4.9 reveal six factors each of which accounts for 68.5% and 75.6% common variance of the 46 and 47 variables relating to budgetees and budget managers respectively. The rotated factor loadings which represent the correlation between the behaviour variable and the factor are used to develop the descriptions and are shown below in parentheses.

Factor I is named 'setting of budget standards' because the variables of high score on this factor reflect the process of setting of budget standards. Budgetees scored positively on variable 2, 'budgetee's private interests are taken into account as much as possible' (.805); variable 17, 'budgeting helps budgetees in knowing exactly which costs they are responsible for' (.590); variable 24, budgetees prefer tight but attainable standards'(.569); and variable 40,'budgetees control over the means of attaining budget standards' (.386). The budgetees scored negatively on variable 33,'budget requires greater efforts on the part of budgetees to attain budget standards' (-.809); variable 34,'budget demands high degree of skill and technical know-how on the part of budgetees in budget performance' (-.592); variable 35,'budgetees get conflicting instructions from different authorities working above them on budget matters' (-.502); variable 30,'budgetees understand fully which part of their budget standards is important than others' (-.458) and the variable 28, 'budget standards for budgetees are quite difficult to attain' (.410). This factor accounts for about 17.6% of the combined variance of all the variables.

On the other hand, budget managers scored positively on variable 2,'private interests of budgetees are taken care of in deciding the budget standards for them' (.718); variable 37,'budget requires greater efforts on the part of budgetees' (.615); variable 35,'budgets set here are quite clear and accurate'(.556); and variable 38,'budgeting requires high degree of skill and technical know-how on the part of the budgetees in attaining budget standards'(.425). Budget managers scored negatively on variable 36,'budgetees prefer budgets that can be easily attained' (-.778); variable 39,'line managers are allowed absolute control over means to attain budget standards' (-.772); variable 34,'budgeting helps line in knowing exactly which costs they are responsible for' (-.679) and variable 12,'line is sufficiently conscious of the need for reliable clerical data'

(-.606). This factor accounts for about 18.7% of the combined variance of all the variables.

However, both budget managers and budgetees scored high on seven variables. These are: goal congruence, knowledge of exact costs, efforts in budget attainments, use of improved skill and technical know-how, budget difficulties, clarity of budget standards and control over means of attaining budget standards.

Factor II is named 'participation in budget-setting' because the variables of high score on this factor reflect the active and influential involvement of budgetees in the activities and interactions associated with the budget process. Budgetees scored positively on variable 20, 'the budget is primarily developed to meet the interests of budgetee's department' (.802); variable 25, 'superiors accept the budgets of budgetees without reservation' (.762); variable 22, 'budgetees exercise high degree of influence in the determination of their budget standards' (.754); and variable 31, 'budgets are finalised with the satisfaction of concerned budgetees' (.687). Budgetees scored negatively on variable 4, 'budgets are set here without taking sufficient account of my department's problems' (-.562); variable 26, 'budgetees have little voice in the development of their budget standards' (-.499); and variable 29, 'budgetees have complete autonomy in making decisions relating to their budget standards' (-.411). This factor accounts for about 12.1% of the combined variance of all the variables.

On the other hand, budget managers scored positively on variable 27, 'budget tends to make budgetees dependent on superiors' (.818); variable 29, 'budgeting gives too much power to financial department' (.567); variable 10, 'superiors ask lines' opinions about matters concerning their areas of work' (.528); and negatively on variable 42, 'staff allows budgetees high degree of influence in the determination of budget standards' (-.689); variable 40, 'budget is not finalised until budgetees are satisfied' (-.677); variable 16, 'budget department is insufficiently consulted in organisational problems' (-.520); variable 42, 'budgetees have favourable attitude towards budgets' (-.491); and variable 30, 'budgeting takes away the freedom of the budgetees' (-.446). This factor accounts for about 15.3% of the combined variance of all the variables.

However, both budget managers and budgetees scored high on four variables. These are: seeking budgetees' opinion on budget matters, consultation of budgetees, influence of budgetees on budget m atter and satisfaction of budgetees with their budget standards.

Factor III is named 'superior-subordinate relationship' in the working of budget system because the variables of high score on this factor reflect budgetee's interactions with their superiors in the attainment of budget standards. Budgetees scored positively on variable 18, 'superiors take personal interest in the budgetary problems of subordinate's departments' (.837); variable 12, 'superiors listen to subordinates' suggestions and complaints with an attitude of fair considerations' (.800); variable 14, 'career opportunities of subordinates depend first of all on budgetees themselves, (.743); variable 42, 'superiors join subordinates in the development of their budget standards' (.725); and negatively on variable 1, 'superiors reject subordinates ideas on budget matters' (-.775); and variable 10, 'superiors working continuously on cost reduction' (-.699). This factor accounts for about 10.5% of the combined variance of all the variables.

On the other hand, budget managers scored positively on variable 26, 'superiors hesitate in taking subordinates co-operation on budget matters (.792); and negatively on variable 24, 'superiors recognise that time and efforts spent in training and educating subordinates by budget managers is an excellent investment' (-.734); variable 23, 'superiors encourage subordinates to use staff effectively' (-.677); variable 25, 'superiors appreciate the suggestions regarding improvements in the production process of organisation' (-.642) and variable 16, 'superiors are sufficiently consulted in the organisational problems' (-.401). This factor accounts for about 11.6% of the combined variance of all the variables.

However, both budget managers and budgetees score high on career opportunities, empathy and co-operation between superior and subordinates on budget matters.

Factor IV is named 'role of line and staff' in the working of budget system because a high score on this factor reflect the staff's role in the development and working of budget system. Line scored positively on variable 37, 'assistance from staff department is available to line on budget matters' (.813); variable 41, 'line discuss with staff whenever problems arise over budget matters' (.720); variable 44, 'staff advice is very helpful in achieving budget standards' (.635); and negatively on variable 6, 'staff take no interest in the goal setting programme of line department' (-.792); variable 13, 'the co-operation between line and staff leaves much to be desired' (-.481) and variable 11, 'people from staff department lack understanding of lines department' (-.475). This factor accounts for about 10% of the combined variance of all the variables.

On the other hand, staff scored positively on variable 1, 'line is ignorant about the job done by staff department' (.813); variable 3, 'staff should leave more to line' (.811); variable 17, 'line do not spend enough efforts to meet production schedules' (.694); variable 14, 'more co-operation is desired between line and staff' (.577); and negatively on variable 7, 'the co-operation between line and staff is smooth' (-.859); variable 4, 'line is insufficiently cost conscious' (-.824); variable 6, 'the first task of my department is service to management' (-.753); variable 13, 'line is convinced of the importance of meeting quality standards' (-.532); variable 18, 'line management follows our advice' (-.441); and variable 20, 'most line managers feel real sense of satisfaction when they attain their budget standards' (-.423). This factor accounts for about 11.5% of the combined variance of all the variables.

However, both budget managers and budgetees scored high on four variables. These are: staff's interest in budgetee's problems, co-operation, understanding and quality of staff advice in the working of budget system.

Factor V is named 'evaluation of budgeted performance' because a high score on this factor reflects the use of budget as an evaluative mechanism of budgetee's performance. Budgetees scored positively on none of the variables; but negatively on variable 39, 'budget evaluation does not concern with human considerations' (-.759); variable 19, 'budgetees attend meetings of top management where budget variances are discussed' (-.737); variable 43, 'superiors never satisfied with budgetees' explanation on budget variances' (-.588); variable 7, 'budgetees performance is appraised on their ability to attain budget standards, (-.568); and variable 16, 'superiors held subordinates personally accountable for budget variances of their department' (-.424). This factor accounts for about 9.4% of the combined variance of all the variables.

On the other hand, budget managers scored positively on variable 47, 'budget variances are considered as factors in the determination of budgetees pay/promotion and career opportunities' (.849); variable 22, 'budgets are yardsticks to evaluate performance' (.811); and negatively on variable 46, 'Line attend meetings where budget variances are discussed' (-.867); variable 45, 'analysis of budget variances is concerned with physical targets' (-.608); and variable 43, 'line managers are personally held accountable for budget variances' (-.459). This factor accounts for about 10.7% of the combined variance of all the variables.

However, budget managers and budgetees scored high on three variables. These are: evaluation of ability vs. traits, self vs. others evaluation and accountability of budget variances in measuring the performance of budgetees.

Factor VI is named 'feedback of performance evaluation' because a high score on this factor reflect the concern with the reporting of performance evaluation to the budgetees by the appraisers. Budgetees scored positively on variable 3, 'the budget reports are sufficiently understandable to budgetees' (.770); variable 23, 'budgetees receive considerable information on their attainments' (.730); and negatively on variable 46, 'superiors encourage free flow of information and ideas among group members on budget matters' (-.824); and variable 32, 'superiors tell subordinates about how well they are doing in term of achieving their budget standards' (-.415). This factor accounts for about 9% of the combined variance of all the variables.

On the other hand, budget managers scored positively on variable 32, 'feedback is limited to areas where adequate performance can be measured' (.853); variable 31, 'reporting of performance evaluation is within the receiver's responsibility' (.744); variable 21, 'feedback of budget information is limited to the behaviours controllable by the budgetees', (.409); variable 33, 'budgetees participate in the feedback sessions' (.404); and negatively on variable 19, 'feedback of performance evaluation closely follows the actions of budgetees' (-.837); variable 11, 'main task of budget variance reports is to show failures of subordinates' (-.477). This factor accounts for about 7.6% of the combined variance of all the variables.

However, budget managers and budgetees both scored high on three variables. These are: reporting, frequency and specificity of performance reports to budgetees.

4.3 ATTITUDE OF BUDGET MANAGERS AND BUDGETEES TOWARDS BUDGET SYSTEMS

The attitude of budget managers and budgetees towards budget system is empirically verified on the basis of four variables. These are: 'budgeting is a tool of accounting control', 'budgeting is a game to play', 'job heavier without standards' and 'prefer to work without standards'. These variables have been adopted on the basis of previous studies (11, 17, 19). The opinion of budget managers and budgetees about these variables that reflect their attitude towards budget system is summarised below in Table 4.10.

TABLE 4.10 **Opinion of Budget Managers and Budgetees Towards the Working of Budget System in the Respective Companies**

Variables of budget system	Response									
	Always		Mostly		Sometimes		Seldom		Never	
	BM	OM	BM	OM	BM	OM	BM	OM	BM	OM
Accounting Control	42	40	20	41	14	13	14	04	13	02
Game to play	37	48	32	40	23	04	05	04	03	04
Heavier with Standards	08	04	16	09	28	23	24	29	24	35
Prefer to work without standards.	56	01	41	10	11	12	-	39	02	38

Table 4.10 reveals that 81% budgetees are of the opinion that budgets are used as a tool of accounting control. This viewpoint is also corroborated by the budget managers (62%). Analysis of data further indicates that budget can be played as a game in the opinion of both budgetees (88%) and budget managers (69%). It means that

both budget managers and budgetees prefer budgeting not only as a tool of accounting control but also as a Game to play.

The consistency and homogeneity of opinion of budgetees and budget managers about their attitude towards budget system is presented below in Table 4.11.

TABLE 4.11 **Mean, Standard Deviation and Coefficient of Variation of the Variables given in Table 4-10**

Variables of budget system	Mean		S.D.		C.V.	
	BM	OM	BM	OM	BM	OM
Accounting tool	2.38	1.33	1.44	.94	61	51
Game to play	2.06	1.75	1.04	.81	50	46
Job heavier with standards	3.53	3.82	1.26	1.15	36	30
Prefer to work without standards.	1.47	4.07	.56	.97	38	24

Table 4.11 indicates the maximum variability in two variables viz. 'Budget is a tool of accounting control' and 'Budgetees prefer to work with standards' - between the opinions of budget managers and budgetees. It means that both budgetees and budget managers agree that budgeting can be played as a game and job becomes heavy to budgetees without standards.

The intercorrelations among the variables of attitude towards budget system is shown below in Table 4.12.

TABLE 4.12 **Intercorrelations among the Variables of Budgetees and Budget Managers Attitude towards Budget System**

Variables of Budget System	Variables of budget system: Accounting control	Game to play	Job heavier with Standards	Prefer to work without standards
Accounting Control	-	.114	.058	-.035
Game to play	(.080)	-	-.073	.109
Job heavier with standards	(-.100)	(-.020)	-	-.108
Prefer to work without standards	(.109)	(-.086)	(.071)	-

N.B.: Figures given in parentheses pertain to budget managers

Table 4.12 reveals that the correlations among all the variables of attitude towards budget system are not significant even at .05 level of significance in case of both budget managers and budgetees. This indicates that all the four variables are independent and least correlated to each other and hence qualified to judge the attitude of budgetees and budget managers towards budget system.

4.3.1 *BUDGET MANAGERS AND BUDGETEES' ATTITUDE TOWARDS BUDGET SYSTEM AND ITS IMPACT UPON BUDGETEE'S JOB PERFORMANCE*

The opinion of budget managers and budgetees about the relationship between the variables of attitude towards budget system and its impact upon budgetees job performance is presented below in Table 4.13.

TABLE 4.13 **Intercorrelations among the Variables of Attitude of Budgetees and Budget Managers & their Impact Upon Budgetees Job Performance**

Variables of budget system	Variables of Performance			
	Influences	Stimulates	Better work	Instructions, not budgets
Accounting Control	.141 (.116)	.001 (-.025)	.021 (-.002)	.031 (.050)
Game to play	-.021 (.032)	.256* (-.020)	.021 (.057)	.079 (-.269)*
Job heavier with standards	.022 (-.040)	-.031 (-.084)	-.090 (-.390)*	.004 (-.006)
Prefer to work without standards	.085 (-.294)*	-.098 (.220)***	.154*** (.018)	.032 (.030)

N.B.: Figures given in parentheses pertain to B.M.
* <.01 ** <.02 *** <.05

Table 4.13 reveals that the variables of budget system- 'budget is a game to play'- is significantly correlated with the performance variable of budgetees-'budget stimulates budgetees for better performance'- at .01 level of significance. It means that budgetees get stimulated for better performance if budget is played as a game rather than a tool of accounting control only.

In the opinion of budget managers, the variables of budget system- 'job heavier without standards', 'budget is a game to play' and 'budgetees prefer to work with standards'- are significantly correlated with the variables of budgetees' job performance' - 'possible to work better at reduced costs'; 'budgets, not instructions will improve the future performance of budgetees' and 'budget influence budgetees' performance'- at .01 level of significance respectively. This clearly brings out that budgetees preference to work with budgets and play budgeting as a game have direct influence over their performance

4.3.2 *BUDGET MANAGERS AND BUDGETEES' ATTITUDE TOWARDS BUDGET SYSTEM AND ITS IMPACT UPON BUDGETEE'S JOB SATISFACTION*

The opinion of budget managers and budgetees about the relationship between the variables of attitude towards budget system and its impact upon budgetees job satisfaction is summarised below in Table 4.14.

TABLE 4.14 **Intercorrelations among the Variables of Attitude of Budgetees as well as Budget Managers and their Impact upon Budgetees Job Satisfaction**

Variables of Budget system	Job Satisfaction Variables			
	Like	Stress	Enjoy	Pressure
Accounting	.061	.095	.011	.040
Control	(.151)	(.005)	(.199)	(-.031)
Game to play	-.080	.084	.251*	-.006
	(.175)	(-.056)	(.244)**	(-.119)
Job heavier	.021	.038	-.194**	.041
with standards	(-.294)*	(.339)*	(-.388)*	(.195)
Prefer to work	.141	-.078	.062	-.095
without standards	(-.353)*	(-.136)	(-.241)**	(+.266)***

N.B. Figures given in parentheses pertain to B.M.
* < .01 ** < . 02 and *** < . 05

Table 4.14 reveals that the variables of budget system - 'Budget is a game to play' - is significantly correlated with the variable of budgetees job satisfaction - 'budgetees enjoy their jobs' - at .01 level of significance. On the other hand, in case of budget managers the budget attitude variables - 'job heavier without standards' and 'prefer to work with standards' - are significantly correlated respectively with the variables of budgetee's job satisfaction - 'budgetees like the department where they work', 'budgetees do not agitate and get nervous and feel pressure on the job' and 'budgetees enjoy their job while working through budgets'-at .01 level of significance. This means that the liking of budgetees to work with budgets and enjoyment of jobs largely depend upon tension and irritation free atmosphere which is possible only when budgeting is played as a game rather than a tool of accounting control.

4.3.3 *GAME OF BUDGET MOTIVATION*

Analysis of data given in Tables 4.8 and 4.9 indicates that 'free, frank and open discussion between budgetees with their superiors', 'finalisation of budget to budgetees satisfaction' and 'educative staff advice to budgetees over budget matters' are the most crucial factors in playing the game of budgeting in the opinion of budgetees. Corroborating the above opinion of budgetees, budget managers express the need for 'greater control of budgetees over the means of attaining their budget standards', 'use of improved skill and technical know-how', 'clarity of budget standards', 'operational autonomy to budgetees', 'budgetees satisfaction through the attainment of budget standards' and 'minimum directives from head office on budget matters for playing the game of budgeting.

Analysis of data given in Tables 4.11 & 4.12 leads us to conclude that playing the game of budgeting not only stimulates budgetees for better performance but also makes their job more enjoyable in the opinion of both budget managers and budgetees as well.

5

CHARACTERISTICS OF BUDGET SYSTEM

This chapter measures the impact of each input factor - setting of budget standards, participation in budget setting, superior subordinate relationship, co-operation between line and staff on budget matters, evaluation and feedback of performance results - of budget system upon the job performance and job satisfaction of budgetees.

5.1 **SETTING OF BUDGET STANDARDS**

The procedure adopted by the companies under study in setting their budget standards and its impact upon budgetees job performance and job satisfaction is described in this section. It is divided into four parts. Part 5.1.1 is devoted to the budgetary practices followed by the companies in the development of their budget standards. Part 5.1.2 describes the opinion of budget managers and budgetees about the perceived characteristics (See Chapter 4, p. 72) of budget-setting. Part 5.1.3 and 5.1.4 present the impact of perceived characteristics of budget setting upon budgetees' job performance and job satisfaction respectively.

5.1.1 *BUDGET SETTING IN PRACTICE*

The main aspects of budget setting - short term as well as long term - such as preparation, time dimensions, approving authorities, functional areas and procedure are described as under.

PREPARATION

All the twenty companies selected in the sample reported that they prepare short term profit budgets for their respective companies as is shown below in Table 5.1.

TABLE 5.1 **Preparation of Short Term Profit Budgets**

Particulars	No. of Companies
Yes	20
No	--
Formal	18
Informal	2

The analysis of data presented in Table 5.1 reveals that eighteen companies prepare their short term profit budgets in the specified formats and two of them simply discuss the short term profit figure at board's level. The practice of preparing short term profit budgets in writing is followed by the management under the assumption that budgets, if not reduced to writing, can frequently turn out to be vague and may not be precisely communicated.

TIME DIMENSIONS

It is observed from Table 5.2 given below that such budgets are prepared for different periods, for example, six companies prepare on monthly, three on quarterly, two on six-monthly and nine on yearly basis.

TABLE 5.2 **Time Dimensions of Short-Term Profit Budgets**

Period	No. of Companies
Monthly	6
Quarterly	3
Six-monthly	2
Yearly	9
Total	20

It is also noted during the interview with the management that in the case of companies in which budgets are prepared on yearly basis, profit budgets on monthly or quarterly basis were also recognized by management to be necessary.

APPROVING AUTHORITIES

The short-term profit budgets are finally approved at different levels in the companies as is presented below in Table 5.3.

TABLE 5.3 **Approving Authorities of Short-term Profit Budgets in the Companies**

Management Levels	No. of Companies
Chairman/President	5
Board of Directors	11
Executive/Management Committee	3
Director Finance	1
Total	20

As is indicated in Table 5.3, in eleven companies short-term profit budgets are approved by the board of directors, in five companies by the Chairman or President, in one company by the Director-Finance and in three companies at the level of executive committee or management committee designated as budget committee or co-ordination committee. This shows that budgeting gets full support and commitment of top management of the companies included in the sample.

FUNCTIONAL AREAS

In addition to short-term profit budgets, companies also prepare budgets for all other important functional areas such as sales, cash, production etc. Table 5.4 presented below exhibits the functional areas for which short-term budgets are prepared by the companies.

Table 5.4 reveals that sales, expenses, advertising and cash budgets are prepared by all the companies taken in the sample. Further analysis of Table 5.4 shows that cash, capital expenditure and expenses budgets are prepared by finance managers, sales and advertising budgets by marketing managers and production budgets by operating managers in most of the cases.

TABLE 5.4 **Short-term Functional Budgets Prepared by the Companies**

Functional Areas	No. of Companies	Developed by (in most of the cases)
Sales	20	Marketing Managers
Expenses	20	Finance Managers
Production	16	Works/Operating Managers
Capital Expenditure	17	Finance Managers
Raw Material	16	Purchase Managers
Research	11	Works Managers
Advertising	20	Marketing Managers
Cash	20	Finance Managers

PROCEDURE

The procedure adopted by the companies for setting the budget goals is either downward or upward as is shown below in Table 5.5.

TABLE 5.5. **Procedure of Budget Setting**

Procedure	No. of Companies
Top downward	13
Bottom Upward	7
Total	20

Table 5.5 shows that in thirteen companies, higher level management develop the budgets which are made available to the subordinates for their comments and suggestions, if any. In seven companies, subordinate staff develop the budgets which are submitted to higher management for final approval. This implies that top management understands the behavioural implications of non-involvement of budgetees in budget-setting.

From the responses to our questionnaire, we find that all the companies under reference include their short-term profit budgets in the detailed plan of operations and revise them periodically. Ten companies revise their budgets monthly, two quarterly, six half-yearly and two on yearly basis.

PERIODS AND AREAS OF LONG TERM BUDGETS

Long-term budgets are also prepared by the companies. Table 5.6 furnishes the details of areas and the period for which such budgets are prepared.

TABLE 5.6 **Periods and Areas of Long-Term Budgets**

Areas	Periods (in years)							
	No Budgets	1	2	3	4	5	10	Total No. of Companies
Sales	1	3	1	6	-	8	1	20
Capital Expenditure	1	3	1	4	1	8	2	20
Profits	1	5	2	4	-	7	1	20
Research	12	3	-	-	-	4	1	20
Expenses	11	3	1	1	-	3	1	20
Cash	9	5	1	-	1	4	1	20
Rural Development	7	11	1	-	-	-	1	20

Tables 5.6 reveals that in most of the companies, long term budgets are prepared for one, three and five year periods. Among them, twelve companies revise their long budgets on yearly basis and eight as and when the need arises. It indicates the thinking of management that budgeting must not dominate the business and that flexibility in budgetary control must be a basic policy so that 'strait jackets' are not imposed and all opportunities are availed of even though they are not covered by the original budgets.

5.1.2 *OPINION OF RESPONDENT ABOUT PERCEIVED CHARACTERISTICS OF BUDGET-SETTING*

The opinion of budget managers and budgetees about the perceived characteristics of budget setting such as goal-congruence, knowledge of exact costs, efforts , use of skill and technical know-how in budget attainment, tightness and specificity of budget standards are described as under:

GOAL-CONGRUENCE

A critical factor in motivating individuals for better performance within an organisation is goal congruence whereby each individual, while satisfying his own needs, is also motivated to contribute his maximum towards the accomplishment of organisational goals. Goal-congruence requires consideration of the broad-range of human needs–social, ego and self-actualisation - in addition to those that can be satisfied by economic rewards. The response of budget managers and budgetees regarding goal-congruence in budget setting is presented below in Table 5.7.

TABLE 5.7 **Goal-congruence in Budget Setting**

Goal Congruence	Response				
	Budget Managers		Budgetees		
	N	%	N	%	%
Always	36	37 %	4	2 %	-35 %
Mostly	19	20 %	35	21 %	-01 %
Sometimes	15	16 %	36	22 %	-06 %
Seldom	14	14 %	54	34 %	-20 %
Never	13	13 %	34	21 %	-08 %
Total	97	100 %	163	100 %	
$\bar{x}$	3.02		3.65	-.63*	
S.D.	1.24		1.12	-.12	

* < .01

Table 5.7 reveals that about 57% of budget managers take care of the personal interests of budgetees while setting the budget standards for them. On the other hand, it is observed that 77% of the budgetees disagree with the budget managers and state that their personal interests are not taken care of by the top management while setting budget standards. The overall difference between the opinion of budget managers and budgetees about goal congruence is statistically significant at .01 level of significance.

These responses further demonstrate that budget and budgetees in practice are aware of the goal-incongruence problems and realise that what is perceived as good for the individual and the department may not be good for the company as a whole and vice-versa. However, the usual analysis of this problem by the budget staff is that such conflict is very common and the solution to it is in having better managers and not in changing the system.

KNOWLEDGE OF EXACT COSTS:

The opinion of budget managers and budgetees regarding the knowledge of budgeted costs for which budgetees are made responsible is given below in Table 5.8.

TABLE 5.8 **Knowledge of Exact Costs in Budget Setting**

Knowledge of exact costs	Response				
	Budget Managers		Budgetees		Difference
	N	%	N	%	%
Always	54	56%	70	42%	+14%
Mostly	37	38%	72	44%	-06%
Sometimes	05	5%	19	12%	-07%
Seldom	01	1%	02	2%	-01%
Never	-	-	-	-	-
Total	97	100%	163	100%	
$\bar{x}$	1.51		1.71		-.20
S.D.	.65		.72		-.07

Table 5.8 reveals that 94% of the budget managers are of the opinion that the budgets which they prepare convey specific knowledge of budgeted costs to the budgetees for which they are made responsible in the attainment of their budgeted performance. They set specific standards in the operating plans of the respective units/sections or departments for control purposes. This is corroborated by 87% of the operating managers. The overall difference of opinion between budget managers and budgetees regarding the exact knowledge of budgeted costs through budgets is found to be statistically insignificant even at .05 level of significance. This implies that both budgetees and budget managers understand the importance of specific cost standards in preparing the budgets for which budgetees are made responsible.

BUDGETEES' EFFORTS IN BUDGET ATTAINMENT

The opinion of budget managers and budgetees regarding the need for putting greater efforts by budgetees in the attainment of their budgeted performance is summarised below in Table 5.9.

TABLE 5.9 **Budgetees' Efforts in Budget Attainment**

Efforts Through Budgets	Response				
	B.M.		O.M.		Difference
	N	%	N	%	%
Always	32	33%	65	40%	-07%
Mostly	36	37%	67	41%	-04%
Sometimes	10	10%	19	12%	-02%
Seldom	13	14%	08	5%	+9%
Never	06	6%	04	2%	+4%
Total	97	100%	163	100%	
$\overline{x}$	2.26		1.90		+.29
S.D.	1.25		.96		+.29

Data given in Table 5.9 shows that about 70% of the budget managers are of the view that budgets are prepared in the light of efforts which will be required to the budgeted performance. On the other hand, 81% of the budgetees hold the view that top management set the budget standards which require maximum efforts on their part in attainment of their budgeted performance. In spite of that the overall difference between the opinion of budget managers and budgetees relating to extraction of extra efforts through budgets is not found to be significant at .01 level of significance.

USE OF IMPROVED SKILL AND TECHNICAL KNOW-HOW

The responses received from budget managers and operating managers with regard to the application of improved skill and technical know-how by budgetees in the attainment of their budget standards are presented below in Table 5.10.

Table 5.10 **Demand for Improved Skills in Budget Attainment**

Demand for Improved Skill	Response B.M.		O.M.		Difference
	N	%	N	%	%
Always	47	48%	76	47%	+01%
Mostly	32	33%	76	47%	-14%
Sometimes	16	17%	10	5%	+12%
Seldom	1	1%	3	2%	-01%
Never	1	1%	3	2%	-01%
Total	97	100%	163	100%	
$\bar{x}$	1.74		1.72		+.02
S.D.	.90		.81		+.09

Table 5.10 indicates that 81% of the budget managers, while preparing the budget standards demand improved skill and technical know-how on the part of budgetees to perform their budget assignments, while 91% of the operating managers hold the view that improved skill and technical know-how on their part is asked for by the top management in the attainment of their budgeted performance. The overall difference between the opinion of budget managers and budgetees regarding the use of improved skill and technical know-how is found to be statistically insignificant.

BUDGETEES' CONTROL OVER VARIABLES (FACTORS)DETERMINING THE ATTAINMENT OF BUDGET STANDARDS

The opinion of budget managers and budgetees regarding the budgetees control over the means of attaining their budget standards is summarised in Table 5.11.

Table 5.11 will reveal that 80 % of the budget managers express that budgetees have adequate powers to secure the means of which the budget standards can be attained; while 76 % of the budgetees disagree of this opinion and state that they have limited powers of control over the factors on which attainment of their budgeted performance depends. The overall difference between the opinion of budget managers and budgetees regarding power of control over the means of attaining budget performance is found to be statistically significant at .01 level of significance.

TABLE 5.11 **Budgetees Control Over the Means of Attaining Their Budget Standards**

Budgetees' control over the means of budget attainment	B.M.	%	O.M. N	%	Difference %
Always	35	36 %	9	5 %	+31 %
Mostly	43	44 %	31	19 %	+25 %
Sometimes	16	17 %	31	19 %	-02 %
Seldom	3 %	3 %	45	28 %	-25 %
Never	-	-	47	29 %	-29 %
Total	97	100 %	163	100 %	
$\bar{x}$	1.89		3.52		-1.63*
S.D.	.83		1.26		-.43

* < .01

TIGHTNESS OF BUDGET STANDARDS

The opinion of budget managers and budgetees regarding the tightness of budget standards to the budgetees' task is summarised below in Table 5.12.

It will be observed from Table 5.12 that 76% of the budget managers frame easily attainable budgets, whereas 48% of the operating managers are of the opinion that the budget standards laid down are difficult to attain. The overall difference between the opinion of budget managers and budgetees regarding the perceived tightness of budget standards to the budgetees' task is statistically significant at .01 level of significance.

Table 5.12 **Perceived Difficulty in Budget Attainment**

Tightness of budget standards.	Response E.M.		O.M.		Difference
	N	%	N	%	%
Always	10	10 %	36	22 %	-12 %
Mostly	13	14 %	42	26 %	-12 %
Sometimes	11 %	11 %	33	20 %	-09 %
Seldom	32	33 %	31	19 %	+14 %
Never	31	32 %	21	13 %	+19 %
Total	97	100 %	163	100 %	
$\bar{x}$	1.41		2.58		-1.17*
S.D.	1.37		1.28		.09

* < .01

SPECIFICITY OF BUDGET STANDARDS

The opinion of budget managers and budgetees pertaining to the budgetees' clarity of budget standards assigned to budgetees is shown below in Table 5.13.

Table 5.13 will reveal that 86 % of the budget managers consider that budgets are framed in clear and precise terms for operating managers. On the other hand, 87 % of the operating managers do not agree with the opinion expressed by the budget managers and state that budgets assigned to them are not quite specific and precise in terms of their responsibilities. It is also observed that in the absence of specificity, clarity and precision in the budgets, they make their own priorities about what to do. The overall difference between the opinion of the budget managers and budgetees regarding the specificity of budget standards is statistically significant at .01 level of significance.

TABLE 5.13 **Budgetees' Clarity of Their Budget Standards**

Clarity of Budgetees	Response				
	B.M.		O.M.		Difference
	N	%	N	%	%
Always	42	43 %	6	4 %	+39 %
Mostly	42	43 %	14	9 %	+34 %
Sometimes	11	12 %	19	12 %	-
Seldom	-	-	61	37 %	-37 %
Never	2	2 %	63	38 %	-36 %
Total	97	100 %	163	100 %	
$\bar{x}$	1.78		3.01		-1.23 *
S.D.	.91		1.63		-0.72

* < .01

5.1.3 *PERCEIVED CHARACTERISTICS OF BUDGET SETTING & ITS IMPACT UPON BUDGETEES' JOB PERFORMANCE*

The opinion of budget managers about the relationship between perceived characteristics of budget setting and its impact thereof upon budgetees' job performance is summarised below in Table 5.14.

TABLE 5.14 **Budget Managers' Opinion About the Relationship Between Perceived Characteristics of Budget Setting and its Impact thereof upon Budgetees' Job Performance.**

Variables of Budget-setting	Job Performance Variables			
	Influences Productivity	Stimulates Performance	Work at reduced costs	Instructions, not budgets
Goal Congruence	-.121	.137	.033	.071
Cost Consciousness	.039	.078	.108	-.040
Knowledge of exact costs	.012	.311*	.094	.114

Tight Budgets	.159	.086	.173	.094
Easy Budgets	.062	-.091	-.149	-.128
Greater Efforts	.042	.106	-.128	.082
Technical Know-how	.208***	.133	-.096	-.067
Control over Means	.000	.158	-.016	-.059
* < .01 ** < .02 *** < .05				

Table 5.14 indicates that the variable of budgetees' job performance - 'budget stimulates budgetees for better performance'- is significantly correlated with the variable of budget setting - 'budget conveys exact knowledge of budgeted costs' - at .01 level of significance.

Table 5.14 also indicates that budget stimulates budgetees for better performance when budget conveys budgetees knowledge of exact costs for which they are made responsible.

The data presented in Table 5.14 shows that it is the budgets, not the instructions from the top management which is essential for improvement of budgetees' performance.

The opinion of budgetees about the perceived characteristics of budget setting and its impact upon their job performance is presented below in Table 5.15.

TABLE 5.15 **The Opinion of Budgetees about the Relationship Between Perceived Characteristics of Budget Setting and their Job Performance**

Variables of Budget-setting	Performance Variables			
	Influences Productivity	Stimulates Performance	Work better at reduced costs	Instructions, not budgets
Goal-Congruence	.219*	-.052	.121	.122
Knowledge of exact costs	.091	.206*	-.100	-.002
Ambiguous goals	.016	.082	-.100	.014

Easy Budgets	-.098	.123	.170***	.107
Tight but attainable Stds.	-.082	.149	.238*	.118
Priorities of goals	.124	.038	-.084	-.0542
Extra efforts	.180***	.024	-.123	-.133
Technical Know-how	.040	-.037	.197*	-.121
Conflicting instructions	.053	.011	-.015	-.119
Control over means of budget attainments	.355*	-.065	.045	.012

* < .01 ** < .02 *** < .05

Table 5.15 reveals that the variables of budgetees' job performance - 'budget influences budgetees' productivity'; 'budget stimulates budgetees for better performance'; and 'possible to work much better at reduced costs' - are significantly correlated with the variables of budget setting'; 'in corporation of personal interests of budgetees in budget standards'; 'budgetees control over the means of attaining budget standards'; 'knowledge of exact costs'; and 'reasonable tightness of budget standards' - at .01 level of significance respectively. This indicates that goal-congruence, operational autonomy, knowledge of exact costs and reasonable tightness of budget standards not only stimulate budgetees for better performance but also influence them for better performance at reduced costs. Analysis of Table 5.15 further reveals that both budget managers and budgetees hold the view that conveying of exact knowledge of budgeted costs to budgetees through budgets is the crucial factor in stimulating budgetees for better performance.

5.1.4 *PERCEIVED CHARACTERISTICS OF BUDGET SETTING AND ITS IMPACT UPON BUDGETEES' JOB SATISFACTION*

The opinion of budget managers about the relationship between perceived characteristics of budget setting and its impact upon budgetees' job satisfaction is summarised below in Table 5.16.

TABLE 5.16 **Opinion of Budget Managers about the Relationship Between Perceived Characteristics of Budget Setting and its Impact upon Budgetees' Job Satisfaction.**

Variables of budget setting	Variables of job satisfaction			
	Like	Tension	Enjoy	Pressure
Goal-congruence	.223**	.286*	.234**	-.053
Cost-Consciousness	.047	.167	-.146	-.072
Knowledge of Exact Costs	.298*	.012	.061	-.197
Clear Goals	.278*	.066	-.032	-.106
Extra Efforts	.015	-.261*	.097	-.087
Skill and Technical Know-how	.209***	-.292*	.069	-.147
Operational Autonomy	.342*	-.150	.145	-.075
Tight Budgets	-.084	-.015	.088	.255*

* < .01 ** < .02 *** < .05

Table 5.16 indicates that the variables of budgetees job satisfaction - 'budgetees like the department where they work'; 'budgetees enjoy their jobs'; and 'budgetees feel pressure on the jobs'- are significantly correlated with the variables of budget setting - 'knowledge of exact costs', 'clear goals' and 'operational autonomy;' 'goal-congruence', 'extra efforts' and 'use of improved skill and technical know-how'; and 'tight goals' - at .01 level of significance respectively. Analysis of data given in Table 5.16 shows clearly that liking of budgetees of their department depends upon the clarity of budget standards, operational autonomy of budgetees and knowledge of exact costs through budgets in the opinion of budget managers. It is further observed that the enjoyment and pleasures derived by the budgetees from their jobs through budget starts disappearing as soon as budget becomes quite difficult to attain, increased demand for improved skill and technical know-how on budgetees' part to attain their budget performance. Analysis of data presented in Table 5.16 clearly shows that budgetees feel pressure only when their budget standards are too tight to attain them.

The opinion of budgetees about the relationship between perceived characteristics of budget setting and its impact upon their job satisfaction is summarised below in Table 5.17.

TABLE 5.17 **Opinion of Budgetees About the Relationship Between Perceived Characteristics of Budget Setting and its Impact upon Budgetees' Job Satisfaction**

Variables of budget setting	Variables of job satisfaction			
	Like	Agitate	Enjoy	Pressure
Goal-congruence	.109	.109	-.025	-.078
Exact costs	.171***	.188**	-.074	-.019
Clear goals	.095	-.094	.011	-.099
Easy standards	-.050	-.097	.095	-.117
Difficult goals	.044	-.102	-.115	-.011
Conflicting priorities	-.025	-.118	-.057	.063
Efforts	.149	.023	.148	.154***
Skill and Technical Know-how	.070	-.125	-.068	.075
Conflicting instructions	-.122	-.028	-.054	.033
Control over means	.246*	-.265*	.028	.039

* < .01 ** < .02 *** < .05

Table 5.17 reveals that the variables of budgetees' job satisfaction- 'I like the department I work in' and 'budget does not make me agitated and nervous' - are significantly correlated at .01 level of significance respectively with the variable of budget setting - 'budgetees' control over the means of attaining budget standards'. This indicates that budgetees enjoy their jobs when they are allowed to exercise significant control over the means of attaining their budget standards. Operational autonomy keep the budgetees free from pressure on the job. This leads to conclude that budgetees' control over the means of budget attainment is the crucial factor in improving the job satisfaction of budgetees.

5.2 PARTICIPATION IN BUDGET SETTING

Budgetees' participation in the development of budget standards and its impact upon their job performance and job satisfaction forms the subject matter of this section. It contains four parts. Part 5.2.1 is devoted to the influence exercised by the budgetees vis-a-vis others like top management, staff officers etc. in the development of budget standards for operating managers . It also highlights the present role and the desirable role of budgetees in the development of budget standards. Part 5.2.2 states the opinion of budget managers and budgetees pertaining to the perceived characteristics (as identified in Chapter 4, p. 73) of participation in budget setting. Finally, parts 5.2.3 and 5.2.4 describe the budgetees' participation in budget setting and its impact upon their job performance and job satisfaction respectively.

5.2.1 *PARTICIPATION IN BUDGET-SETTING*

The major issues pertaining to budgetees' participation in budget-setting are discussed as under.

AREAS OF OPERATION

The opinion of operating managers regarding the areas of operations which demand their maximum attention in attaining their budgeted performance is presented below in Table 5.18.

TABLE 5.18 **Ranking of Operations Demanding Attention of Budgetees**

Areas of Operation	Budgetees Response	
	N	%
Leading the personnel	09	05 %
Fulfilling the production schedule	18	11 %
Maintaining the quality	49	30 %
Keeping the cost down	83	51 %

Developing new product and processes	04	3%
Total	163	100 %

Analysis of results given in Table 5.18 reveals that maximum attention (51%) of budgetees is demanded by top management to keep down the cost of products. Operating managers rank maintenance of quality, fulfilling the production schedules in time, leading the personnel and development of new product and process in that order demanding their attention by the top management. This indicates that cost and quality control are the two most important areas where operating managers' maximum attention is demanded.

CONTROL OVER BUDGETED COSTS

The opinion of operating managers regarding their influence on budgeted costs through budgets is summarised below in Table 5.19.

TABLE 5.19 **Budgetees' Control Over the Costs that Influence Their Efficiency of Budget Performance**

	Degree of Influence									
Costs	Maximum		Moderate		Minimum		Not at all		Total	
	N	%	N	%	N	%	N	%	N	%
Raw Material	41	25 %	45	28 %	36	22 %	41	25 %	163	100 %
Labour Costs	11	7 %	17	10 %	61	37 %	74	46 %	163	100 %
Research Costs	4	3 %	49	30 %	76	47 %	34	20 %	163	100 %
Factory Costs	7	4 %	5	3 %	78	48 %	73	45 %	163	100 %
Adm. Costs	3	2 %	50	31 %	67	41 %	43	26 %	163	100 %
Selling Costs	56	35 %	76	47 %	23	14 %	8	4 %	163	100 %

Table 5.19 indicates that budgetees have partial control over the budgeted costs for which they are made responsible through budgets. As is evident from Table 5.19 that 25 % control is exercised

by the operating managers over the raw material costs which normally constitutes the largest proportion of the total cost of production.

OPERATING STANDARDS

Budgetees' opinion pertaining to their influence over the operating efficiency of their own department is presented below in Table 5.20.

TABLE 5.20 **Budgetees' Influence over the Budgeted Efficiency of Budget Performance**

Influences over Efficiency	Response (Budgetees)	
	N	%
Yes	139	85 %
No	24	15 %

Table 5.20 indicates that 85 % of the operating managers are of the opinion that their operating efficiency can be influenced by them provided they get the opportunity. But on the other hand, it is observed from Table 5.21 summarised below that only 10 % influence is exercised by them in attaining their budgeted performance. Rest 90 % lies with the others - Seniors (58 %), Staff (24 %) and Juniors (8 %).

TABLE 5.21 **Contribution of Managerial Personnel Towards Efficiency of Budget Performance**

	Degree of Influence									
People	Maximum		Moderate		Minimum		Not at all		Total	
	N	%	N	%	N	%	N	%	N	%
Seniors	95	58 %	37	23 %	16	10 %	15	09 %	163	100%
Budgetees	16	10 %	63	38 %	76	47 %	08	05 %	163	100%
Staff	39	24 %	56	35 %	39	23 %	29	18 %	163	100%
Juniors	13	08 %	07	04 %	32	20 %	111	68 %	163	100%
Total	163	100 %	163	100 %	163	100 %	163	100 %	163	100%

TECHNICAL STANDARDS

The influence of budgetees as well as others on technical standards is shown below in Table 5.22.

TABLE 5.22 **Influence of Various People on Technical Standards**

People	Degree of Influence Maximum		Moderate		Minimum		Not at all		Total	
	N	%	N	%	N	%	N	%	N	%
Seniors	23	14 %	83	51 %	34	21 %	23	14 %	163	100%
Budgetees	06	4 %	05	03 %	79	48 %	73	45 %	163	100%
Financial Staff	17	10 %	48	29 %	37	24 %	61	37 %	163	100%
Technical Staff	117	72 %	27	17 %	13	07 %	06	04 %	163	100%
Total	163	100 %	163	100 %	163	100 %	163	100 %	163	100%

Table 5.22 indicates that the situation with regard to technical standards is also not good. It is clear from Table 5.22 that only 4 % influence is exercised by the operating managers and the rest 96 % by others, i.e., top management (72 %), Financial Staff (10 %), and Seniors (14 %). Hence it leads to conclude that operating managers exercise minimum control over both operating as well as technical standards assigned to them.

ACTUAL AND DESIRABLE PARTICIPATION

The relationship between a series of participation situations in budget-setting by the operating managers and the extent to which they were encouraged to participate in decision-making is presented below in Table 5.23. Participation is not characterised in terms of either as dichotomy nor even the degree of overall influence, but rather as a continuum of decision behaviours ranging from a manager making his own decisions without explanation or prior consultation at one end of the scale to complete delegation at the other end.

TABLE 5.23 **Actual and Desirable Role of Budgetees as Desired by them in Budget-Setting**

PARTICIPATION CONTINUUM	Role of Budgetees Actual		Desirable	
	N	%	N	%

Decision taken by operating managers without staff consultation	-	-	-	-
Decision taken by operating managers with staff consultation	06	4 %	31	18 %
Decision taken by budget managers without operating managers' consultation	35	20 %	-	-
Decision taken by budget managers with operating managers' consultation	11	7 %	27	17 %
Proposed by operating managers and operating managers' opinions prevail	02	1 %	3	2 %
Proposed by operating managers but budget managers' opinions generally prevail	01	1 %	07	4 %
Proposed by staff and their opinions generally prevail	30	18 %	04	3 %
Proposed by staff but operating managers' opinions prevail	02	1 %	03	2 %
Proposed by operating managers decision made jointly	04	3 %	37	22 %
Proposed by budget managers decision made jointly	03	2 %	29	18 %
Proposed by others and their opinions have a lot of weight	29	17 %	01	1 %
Proposed by others but opera-ting managers' opinion has a lot of weight	01	1 %	03	2 %
Proposed by operating managers and their opinion has a lot of weight	01	1 %	16	10 %
Proposed by operating managers but budget managers' opinion has a lot of weight	14	9 %	02	1 %
Operating managers' opinions are not asked by budget mana-gers but decisions are communicated	21	13 %	-	-
Budget managers' opinion are not asked but decisions are communicated to them	01	1 %	-	-
Operating managers' opinions are not asked and decisions are also not communicated	02	1 %	-	-
Budget managers opinions are not asked and decisions are not explained to budget managers	-	-	-	-
Total	163	100 %	163	100 %

Table 5.23 reveals the opinion of operating managers about their involvement in budget-setting through the following statements:

Decision taken by budget managers without budgetees consultation (20 %)

Proposed by budget managers and their opinion prevails in standard-setting (18 %)

Proposed by others, and their opinion has a lot of weight (17 %)

Operating managers' opinions are not asked by budget managers but decisions are explained to operating managers (13 %)

Proposed by operating managers but budget managers' opinions have a lot of weight (9 %)

Above statements indicate that major role is played by the top management, budget managers and technical staff in developing the budgets for operating managers. Even if they are sometimes involved in budget-setting, they are not in a position to exercise enough influence over their seniors.

Regarding the desirable role of budgetees, the following statements of budgetees are worth noting.

Proposed by operating managers but decisions are made jointly (22 %)

Decision taken by operating managers with staff consultation (19 %)

Proposed by them but decisions are made jointly (18 %)

Decision taken by them with operating manager's consultation (17 %)
Proposed by operating managers and operating managers have a lot of weight (10 %)

The above statements indicate the increased desire of budgetees to exercise more influence in the decisions pertaining to budget-setting for their departments.

5.2.2 *RESPONDENTS' OPINION TOWARDS PERCEIVED CHARACTERISTICS OF PARTICIPATION IN BUDGET-SETTING*

The respondent's opinion about perceived characteristics of participation in budget-setting - opinion, consultation, influence and acceptance - is discussed as under.

OPINION ON BUDGET MATTERS

Table 5.24 presents below the opinion of budget managers and budgetees regarding the opinion sought from the budgetees by the top management over the problems of their areas of work while setting the budgets for them.

Table 5.24 **Budgetees Opinion Sought While Developing the Budget Standards**

Budgetees' opinion	Responses				Difference
	B.M.		O.M.		
	N	%	N	%	%
Always	38	39 %	61	37 %	+2 %
Mostly	43	45 %	66	40 %	+5 %
Sometimes	10	10 %	28	17 %	-7 %
Seldom	05	5 %	04	3 %	+2 %
Never	01	1 %	04	3 %	-2 %
Total	97	100 %	163	100 %	
$\bar{x}$	1.80		1.74		+.06
S.D.	.85		.89		-.04

Table 5.24 indicates that the statistical difference between the opinion of budget managers and budgetees in seeking the budgetees' opinion pertaining to their area of work while setting the budget standards is insignificant even at .05 level of significance.

CONSULTATION ON BUDGET MATTERS

The opinion of budget managers and budgetees with regard to

consultation with budgetees in budget setting is presented below in Table 5.25.

TABLE 5.25 **Consultation with Budgetees in Budget Setting**

Consultation with budgetees	Budget Managers N	Budget Managers %	Budgetees N	Budgetees %	Difference %
Always	38	39 %	08	5 %	+34 %
Mostly	43	45 %	30	18 %	+27 %
Sometimes	10	10 %	43	26 %	-16 %
Seldom	05	5 %	49	30 %	-25 %
Never	01	1 %	33	21 %	-20 %
Total	97	100 %	163	100 %	
$\bar{x}$	1.90		3.48		-1.58*
S.D.	.85		1.14		-.29

* < .01

The difference between the opinion of budget managers and budgetees with regard to the consultation with budgetees while setting budgets is statistically significant at .01 level of significance. As is clear from Table 5.25 that 84 % of the budget managers stated that budgetees are consulted while setting the budgets for their own departments, whereas 51 % of the budgetees refuted the above statement of budget managers.

INFLUENCE ON BUDGET-SETTING

Table 5.26 presents below the opinion of operating managers and budgetees about the budgetees' influence in budget-setting.

TABLE 5.26 **Budgetees' Influence in the Setting of their Own Budgets**

Budgetees' influence	Budget managers N	Budget managers %	Budgetees N	Budgetees %	Difference in %
Always	41	42 %	07	4 %	+38 %
Mostly	28	29 %	16	10 %	+19 %
Sometimes	13	14 %	30	18 %	-4 %
Seldom	04	4 %	61	43 %	-39 %
Never	11 %	11 %	41	25 %	-14 %
Total	97	100 %	163	100 %	
$\bar{x}$	1.11		2.26		-1.15*
S.D.	1.22		1.07		+.15

* < .01

Analysis of Table 5.26 reveals that 71 % of budget managers allow budgetees to exercise high degree of influence in the setting of their budget standards. On the other hand, 68 % of the budgetees disagree with the above opinion of budget managers. The statistical difference between the opinion of budget managers and budgetees regarding budgetees influence in setting their budget standards is significant at .01 level of significance.

BUDGETEES SATISFACTION TO THEIR BUDGET STANDARDS

Budgetees acceptance to the final budgets assigned to them is one of the most critical aspect of the participation in budget setting. The opinion of budget managers and budgetees about the satisfaction of budgetees to their budget standards is summarised below in Table 5.27.

TABLE 5.27 **Development of Budgets to the Budgetees' Satisfaction**

B..dgetees' satisfaction	Responses				
	Budget Manager		Budgetees		Difference
	N	%	N	%	%
Always	23	24 %	10	6 %	+ 18 %
Mostly	26	27 %	10	6 %	+ 21 %
Sometimes	22	23 %	13	7 %	+ 16 %
Seldom	18 %	18 %	76	46 %	-28 %
Never	08	8 %	54	34 %	-26 %
Total	977	100 %	163	100 %	-
$\bar{x}$	2.58		4.06		-1.48*
S.D.	1.22		1.10		.12

* < .01

The Table 5.27 indicates that 51 % of the budget managers are of the opinion that operating managers' budgets are not finalised unless they are satisfied with them. On the other hand, 81 % of the budgetees do not corroborate the opinion of budget managers and state that budgets are made to the satisfaction of top management only. The difference between the opinion of budget managers and budgetees regarding the finalisation of budgets upto the budgetees' satisfaction is statistically significant at .01 level of significance.

5.2.3 *PARTICIPATION AND BUDGETEES' JOB PERFORMANCE*

The opinion of budget managers about the relationship between perceived characteristics of budgetees' participation in budget-setting and its impact upon budgetees' job performance is shown below in Table 5.28.

TABLE 5.28 **Relationship Between Perceived Characteristics of Participation and Budgetees' Job Performance**

Participation Variables	Job Performance Variables			
	Influences Productivity	Stimulates Performance	Work better at reduced costs	Instructions, not budgets
Insufficient consultation	-.15716***	-.05327	-.10131	.19681
Satisfaction	.04436	.00084	-.12602	.24308**
Influence	.11754	.03765	.29294*	.06823
Attitude	.32952*	.36231*	-.12311	.10227
Opinion	.05675	-.01089	-.07922	-.06365

*< .01 ** < .02 ***< .05

Table 5.28 indicates that the participation variable – 'favourable attitude of budgetees' - is significantly correlated with the budgetees' performance variables - 'budget stimulates for better performance' and 'budget influences budgetees' productivity' - at .01 level of significance. Another performance variable - 'possible to work much better at reduced costs' - is also significantly correlated with the participation variable - 'budgetees exercise high degree of influence in the determination of their budget standards' - at .01 level of significance.

The opinion of budgetees about the relationship between perceived characteristics of participation in budget setting and their impact upon their job performance is summarised below in Table 5.29.

TABLE 5.29 **Relationship Between Perceived Characteristics of Participation and Budgetees Job Performance**

Participation Variables	Performance Variables			
	Influences Productivity	Stimulates Performance	Work better at reduced costs	Instructions, not budgets
Insufficient consultation	-.022	-.006	.025	.077
Satisfaction	.132	-.071	-.116	.016
Influence	.044	-.055	.202***	.013
Opinion	.059	-.019	-.120	-.063
Acceptance	-.003	.095	.060	-.009
Interest	.038	.075	-.022	.063
Little Voice	-.130	-.166	.024	-.028
Complete autonomy	-.066	.032	-.015	.068
Control	.099	.063	-.079	-.022

*** < .05

Table 5.29 shows that the participation variable - 'budgetees exercise high degree of influence in budget setting of their departments' - is significantly correlated with the performance variable - 'possible to work better at reduced costs' - at .05 level of significance. This indicates that when budgetees are permitted to exercise enough influence in setting their budget standards results in more effective performance at reduced costs.

It leads to conclude that both budget managers and operating managers are of the opinion that influence of budgetees in their budget setting is the most significant factor to improve the performance of budgetees.

5.2.4 *PARTICIPATION AND BUDGETEES' JOB SATISFACTION*

The opinion of budget managers with regard to the relationship between perceived characteristics of participation in budget setting and its impact upon budgetees' job satisfaction is summarised below in Table 5.30.

TABLE 5.30 **Relationship Between Perceived Characteristics of Participation in Budget Setting and Budgetees' Job Satisfaction**

Participation Variables	Job Satisfaction Variables			
	Like	Agitate	Enjoy	Pressure
Insufficient consultation	-.23676*	.16927***	-.15802***	-.07053
Budgetees' Satisfaction	.03225	-.08886	.11766	-.26914*
Budgetees' Influence	.06899	.14682	.01879	.06945
Budgetees' Attitude	.13599	-.27489*	.31198*	-.15575***
Budgetees' Opinion	.20864*	-.00304	.15181***	.11873

* < .01 ** < .02 *** < .05

Table 5.30 indicates that budgetees job satisfaction variables - 'Budgetees enjoy their job' and 'budgetees like the department where they work' - are significantly correlated with participation variables - 'favourable attitudes towards participation', 'sufficient consultation' , and 'superiors ask budgetees' opinion over budget matters' - at .01, .02 and .05 level of significance respectively. This indicates that favourable attitude of budgetees towards participation is an important factor in making their job enjoyable to them. Budget managers also feel that sufficient consultation of budgetees over their budget matters improve their liking towards budget standards and hence job satisfaction.

Table 5.30 further reveals that budgetees feel nervous when they are allowed to participate in their budget setting but they are reluctant to participate.

Finally, budgetees feel pressure when budget is not finalised upto their satisfaction and just communicated to them.

The opinion of budgetees about the relationship between perceived characteristics of participation in budget setting and its impact upon their job satisfaction is summarised below in Table 5.31.

TABLE 5.31 **Relationship Between Participation and Budgetees Job Satisfaction**

Participation Variables	Job Satisfaction Variables			
	Like	Agitate	Enjoy	Pressure
Insufficient consultation	-.07057	.17096***	.00514	.04948
Opinion	.05389	.05216	-.03645	-.14355
Interest	.07755	.09507	-.02073	.02556
Influence	.09466	-.11138	.00165	.14491
Complete autonomy	-.06819	.06247	-.12346	-.03106
Little Voice	-.16254***	.03769	-.03368	.07764
Satisfaction	-.06175	-.03553	.01076	.01876
Control	-.06236	.10438	-.04338	.15209
Acceptance	.09851	.11585	-.10024	-.00929

*** < .05

Analysis of results given in Table 5.31 indicates that none of the variables of participation is significantly correlated with budgetees' job satisfaction variables at .01 level of significance. However, it is observed that the job satisfaction variables - 'budgetees like the department where they work' and 'budget makes budgetees agitated and nervous' - are significantly correlated with the participation variables - 'little voice' and 'insufficient consultation over budget problems' - at .05 level of significance . It means that whenever there is little or no voice of budgetees in their budget setting, their job satisfaction starts disappearing. It is also observed that budgetees feel agitated and nervous when they are insufficiently consulted on the departmental problems while setting their budget standards.

5.3 SUPERIOR -SUBORDINATE RELATIONSHIP

The relationship of budgetees with their superiors in the working of budget system and its impact upon budgetees' job performance and satisfaction is described in this section. It contains four parts. Part 5.3.1. is devoted to the superior-subordinate relationship during the working of budget system in the companies under study, Part 5.3.2 presents the opinion of budget managers and subordinates (Budgetees) about perceived characteristics of superior-subordinate relationships (as identified in Chapter 4, and finally, the relationship between perceived characteristics of superior. Subordinate relationships and its impact upon subordinates' job performance and job satisfaction are described in Parts 5.3.3. and 5.3.4 respectively.

5.3.1 *SUPERIOR-SUBORDINATE RELATIONSHIPS IN PRACTICE*

The budgetees relationship with their superiors in terms of frequency of interaction, purposes and desirable role in meetings over budget matters is described as under.

FREQUENCY OF MEETINGS

The frequency of budgetees' meetings with their superiors over budget matters in the companies under study is presented in Table 5.32.

TABLE 5.32 **Frequency of Meetings Between Superiors and Subordinates over Budget Matters.**

Frequency	Response	
	N	%
Daily	34	21 %
Weekly	37	23 %
Monthly	12	7 %
Yearly	8	5 %
As Needed	72	44 %
Total	163	100 %

Table 5.32 shows that in 44 % cases, superior-subordinate meetings are held as and when needed without advance preparation. It is also observed that interaction between superior and subordinates over budget matters takes place daily and weekly only in 21 % and 23 % cases respectively.

PURPOSE OF MEETINGS

Table 5.33 given below presents the purpose for which meetings are held between the budgetees and their superiors.

TABLE 5.33 **Purpose of Meetings Held Between Superior and Subordinates Over Budget Matters**

Purpose of meetings	Response	
	N	%
Communication of budgetees' feelings to superiors	13	8 %

Perceiving effects of Budgetees behaviour on superiors	17	10 %
Perceiving effect of superiors' behaviour on budgetees	29	18 %
Hearing superiors and accepting their criticism	56	35 %
Appropriately interacting with superiors over budget matters	11	6 %
Formality	37	23 %
Total	163	100 %

Table 5.33 reveals that the purpose of 35 % meetings held between subordinates and their superiors is only to listen to the superiors over budget matters. Further analysis of Table 5.33 indicates that the purpose of 23 %, 18 %, and 10 % of the meetings are to communicate superior's decisions to subordinates, perceived effects of superior's behaviour on budgetees, and perceive the effect of budgetees' behaviour on superiors respectively. Budgetees get appropriate interaction with superiors over budget matters only in 8 % and 6 % cases respectively.

DESIRABLE ROLE OF MEETINGS

The opinion of budgetees about the desirable purpose of subordinates' meetings with their superiors is summarised below in Table 5.34.

TABLE 5.34 **Desirable Purpose of the Meetings Held Between the Budgetees and Their Superiors.**

Desirable purpose of meetings	Response N	%
Meaningful interaction between superiors and subordinates	9	5 %
Securing a respectable place in the eyes of subordinates	4	3 %
Understanding dynamic complexities in subordinates behaviour	7	4 %
Developing diagnostic skills to understand subordinates' problems	67	41 %
Acquire skill of helping subordinates on budget matters	76	47 %
Formality	-	-
Total	163	100 %

Table 5.34 shows that 41 % and 47 % subordinates are of the opinion that the purpose of such meetings should be to understand

the budget problems and help the subordinates by their superiors over budget matters respectively, so that they can achieve their targets effectively. It is also observed that no meetings should be held only for the sake of formality.

5.3.2 *RESPONDENT'S OPINION ABOUT PERCEIVED CHARACTERISTICS OF SUPERIOR-SUBORDINATE RELATIONSHIPS*

The opinion of budgetees and budget managers about perceived characteristics of superior-subordinate relationships - career opportunities of subordinates, consideration of superiors towards subordinate's need and feelings and co-operation of superiors towards their subordinates - is discussed as under.

CAREER OPPORTUNITY

The opinion of budgetees and budget managers about the association between subordinates' career opportunities and their budgeted performance is presented below in Table 5.35

TABLE 5.35 **Respondents' Opinion About the Relationship Between Career Opportunities of Budgetees and Budgeted Performance**

Association of Career Opportunities with Budgeted Performance	Response				
	Budget managers		Budgetees		Differences
	N	%	N	%	%
Always	37	38 %	4	3 %	+35 %
Mostly	31	32 %	9	5 %	+27 %
Sometimes	16	17 %	8	5 %	+12 %
Seldom	6	6 %	67	41 %	-35 %
Never	7	7 %	75	46 %	-39 %
Total	97	100 %	163	100 %	
$\bar{x}$	2.12		3.80		-1.68*
S.D.	1.20		1.34		-.14

* < .01

Analysis of Table 5.35 reveals that 70 % of the budget managers are of the opinion that the pay, promotion and career opportunities of subordinates are not associated with their budgeted performance. Subordinates are free to avail better pay, promotion and career opportunities in the company concerned or outside the organisation. On the other hand, 87 % of the budgetees hold the view that their pay, promotion and career opportunities in the company is decided by their superiors on the basis of their budgeted performance. The difference between the opinion of budget managers and subordinates about the association of career opportunities with their budgeted performance is statistically significant at .01 level of significance.

EMPATHY

The opinion of budgetees and budget managers about superiors' concern about the needs and feelings of subordinates over budget matters is presented below in Table 5.36.

TABLE 5.36 **Opinion of Budget Managers and Budgetees Pertaining to Superior's Concern About Subordinates' Needs and Feelings Over Budget Mat ters**

Superiors empathy towards subordinates	Response				
	Budget managers		Subordinates		Difference
	N	%	N	%	%
Always	46	48 %	41	25 %	+23 %
Mostly	33	34 %	56	35 %	-1 %
Sometimes	14	14 %	33	21 %	-7 %
Seldom	1	1 %	20	12 %	-11 %
Never	3	3 %	13	7 %	-4 %
Total	97	100 %	163	100 %	
$\bar{x}$	1.53		2.44		-.91***
S. D.	.90		1.22		-.32

*** < .05

Table 5.36 shows that 82 % of the superiors are always supportive, friendly and helpful to subordinates in the attainment of their budgeted performance effectively. On the other hand, 44 % of the budgetees do not corroborate the opinion expressed by their superiors. The difference between the opinion of budget managers and subordinates regarding the superiors' attitude towards the needs and feelings of subordinates is statistically significant only at .05 level of significance.

CO-OPERATION

The views expressed by budgetees and budget managers about the superiors' co-operation to their subordinates over budget matters is presented below in Table 5.37.

TABLE 5.37 **Co-operation Between Superior and Subordinates Over Budget Matters**

Superiors co-operation to subordinates	Response: Budget managers N	Budget managers %	Subordinates N	Subordinates %	Difference %
Always	31	32 %	2	1 %	+31 %
Mostly	33	34 %	7	4 %	+30 %
Sometimes	22	23 %	46	28 %	-5 %
Seldom	8	8 %	59	36 %	-28 %
Never	3	3 %	49	31 %	-28 %
Total	97	100 %	163	100 %	
$\bar{x}$	1.85		3.90		-2.05*
S.D.	1.22		1.92		-.70

*< .01

Table 5.37 reveals that 68 % budget managers think that superiors extend necessary co-operation to their subordinates over budget problems. On the other hand, 67 % of the subordinates state that sufficient co-operation is not extended by the superiors in attaining their budgeted performance. This indicates that superiors are not very co-operative to their subordinates in handling the operational problems. The overall difference between the opinion of budgetees and budget managers regarding superiors' co-operation with their subordinates over budget problem is statistically significant at .01 level of significance.

5.3.3 *SUPERIOR-SUBORDINATE RELATIONSHIPS AND ITS IMPACT UPON SUBORDINATES' BUDGETED PERFORMANCE.*

The opinion of budget managers about the relationship between perceived characteristics of superior-subordinate relationship and its impact upon budgetees' job performance is summarised below in Table 5.38.

TABLE 5.38 **Superior-Subordinate Relationships and its Impact upon Subordinate's Job Performance**

Variables of Superior-Subordinate relationships	Subordinate's Performance Variables Influences Productivity	Stimulates Performance	At reduced costs	Instructions
Career opportunities	-.06173	-.14052	-.05278	.07376
Use of Staff	.23121**	.02681	.09945	-.02534
Training and education	-.4739	-.15798	.20539***	-.16082
Appreciation of suggestions	.25275*	.08259	.17101	-.01345
Empathy	-.27011*	.25754*	.11222	-.04873

* < .01   ** < .02   *** < .05

Table 5.38 reveals that in the opinion of superiors, subordinates' performance variable - 'Budget Influences budgetees performance' - is significantly correlated with the variables and perceived characteristics of superior subordinate relationships - 'Boss appreciates the suggestions over budget matters' and 'boss co-operates with his subordinates on budget problems'; 'subordinates are encouraged to use staff effectively' - at .01 and .02 level of significance respectively. The table further discloses that subordinate's stimulation for better performance is significantly correlated at .01 level of significance with 'superior's co-operation with subordinates without delay and hesitation over budget matters'. This indicates that budget managers also realise the importance of superiors' co-operation, appreciation and help to budgetees over budget matters in influencing and stimulating their job performance.

Table 5.39 presents below the opinion of budgetees about the perceived characteristics of superior-subordinate relationships and its impact upon subordinate's (budgetees) job performance.

TABLE 5.39 **Superior-Subordinate Relationship and its Impact upon Budgetees Job Performance**

Superior-subordinate relationship variables	Subordinates' performance variables Influences productivity	Stimulates performance	At reduced costs	Instructions, not budgets
Rejection of ideas	.11268	.04114	.10830	.12443
Emphasis on cost reduction	.16059***	-.04584	-.06574	-.12935
Listen to suggestions	.03402	.194404**	-.21158*	.15258***
Career opportunities	.20155*	.11001	.08848	-.09135
Personal example	.19434**	-.07803	-.01631	.04870
Dictate goals	-.05605	-.15443***	.20350*	.05699
Joins in developing budgets	.13539	-.13504	-.01294	-.00647

* < .01 *** < .05

Table 5.39 reveals that subordinates' performance variable - 'Budget influence budgetees performance' - is significantly correlated with the variables of perceived characteristics of superior-subordinate relationships - 'Boss is working continuously on cost reduction', 'career opportunities depends first of all on budgetees themselves' and 'superiors put personal examples of performing the job' - at .01, .02, .05 level of significance respectively. This indicates that budget influences budgetees' performance, if pay, promotion and career opportunities are decided independently.

Analysis of Table 5.39 further reveals that subordinates can work better at reduced costs provided superiors listen to the subordinate's suggestions, give fair consideration and sell their ideas to subordinates rather than dictate them. Both the variables are significantly correlated with the variables of job performance at .01 level of significance.

5.3.4 *SUPERIOR- SUBORDINATE RELATIONSHIPS AND ITS IMPACT UPON SUBORDINATES' JOB SATISFACTION*

The opinion of budget managers about the relationship between perceived characteristics of superior-subordinate relationships and its impact upon budgetees' job satisfaction is presented below in

Table 5.40.

TABLE 5.40. **Relationship Between Budgetees Job Satisfaction and Superior-Subordinate Relationships**

Superior-Subordinate Relationship Variables	Job Satisfaction			
	Like	Enjoy	Stress	Pressure
Career opportunity	.10285	-.13942	.05084	-.34461*
Use of staff	.08027	-.02727	.02610	.06274
Training and eucation	-.04389	.13487	-.06085	.15706
Appreciation of suggestions	.10341	-.08343	.22022***	-.02458
Co-operation	-.12824	.48131*	-.17778	.12583

* < .1 *** < . 05

Table 5.40 shows that the variables of superior-subordinate relationships - 'association of career opportunities with budgeted performance' and 'cooperation between superior and subordinates' - are found to be significantly correlated at .01 level of significance with the job satisfaction variables - 'Feeling of stress' and 'pressure' and 'budgetees enjoy their jobs'. This indicates that superiors' co-operation with their subordinates in the attainment of their budget standards made jobs more enjoyable to the budgetees. However, association of career opportunities to the budget performance of budgetees put them under pressure on the job.

Table 5.41 presents below the opinion of Budgetees about the perceived characteristics of superior-subordinate relationship and its impact upon their job satisfaction.

TABLE 5.41 **Perceived Characteristics of Superior-Subordinate Relationships and its Impact Upon Subordinate's Job Satisfaction.**

Variables	Job Satisfaction Variables			
	Like	Enjoy	Stress	Pressure
Rejection of Ideas	-.01372	.03902	-.11834	.21934*
Cost reduction	.07245	-.02152	.01890	.03637
Appreciation of Suggestions	.02971	.03721	-.01482	-.07228
Career Opportunity	.17588**	-.05414	-.14704	.05812

Personal Example	.00723	.00852	.08453	-.01551
Dictate Ideas	.05954	.04398	.06159	.07893
Joint Development of Budgets	-.03377	.02287	.05016	.04361

* < .01 **< .02

Table 5.41 indicates that superior-subordinate relationship variables - 'rejection of ideas by superiors' and 'career opportunities' - are significantly correlated with job satisfaction variables of subordinates - 'budgetees feel pressure in their job' and 'budgetees like the department where they work' - at 01 and .02 level of significance respectively.

This indicates that rejection of subordinate's suggestions by their superiors over budget matters put them under pressure resulting in their job dissatisfaction. Table 5.41 further reveals that liking of budgetees of their jobs is improved when their pay, promotion and career opportunities are kept delinked from their budgeted performance.

5.4 ROLE OF LINE AND STAFF IN BUDGET SYSTEM

The role of staff (budget managers/industrial engineers) in the working of budget system is described in this section. It contains four parts. The interactions between line (budgetees) and staff over budget matters is described in Part 5.4.1. Part 5.4.2 is devoted to the respondents views relating to the perceived characteristics (as identified in Chapter-4, page 74 of staff's role in budget system. The relationship between perceived role of staff in budget system and its impact upon budgetee's job performance and job satisfaction is presented in Parts 5.4.3 and 5.4.4 respectively

5.4.1 *STAFF'S ROLE IN BUDGET SYSTEM*

The role of staff in terms of their influence, participation, communication and relationship with line in the working of budget system followed by the companies in the sample is described as under.

INFLUENCE

The opinion of line managers regarding staff's influence in the working of their departments is presented below in Table 5.42.

TABLE 5.42 Influence of Budget Department on Budgetees' Working

	Degree of Influence							
Departments	Maximum		Moderate		Minimum		Total	
	N	%	N	%	N	%	N	%
Engineering	83	51 %	54	34 %	26	15 %	163	100 %
Finance	07	4 %	13	8 %	143	88 %	163	100 %
Personnel	32	20 %	04	3 %	127	77 %	163	100 %
Budget	78	48 %	68	42 %	17	10 %	163	100 %

Table 5.42 indicates that the engineering department followed by the budget department has the maximum influence over the budgetees in the opinion of 48 % of line managers. It is also clear from the table that the influence of finance and personnel department over budgetees is almost insignificant.

PARTICIPATION

The data relating to staff's participation in the finalisation of budgets is presented below in Table 5.43.

TABLE 5.43 Staff's Participation in Budget Finalisation

Staff's Role in Budget Sessions	No. of Companies
Primarily staff with some line assistance	1
Primarily line with some staff assistance	1
Line and staff participating on equal basis	14
Staff personnel only	2
Line personnel only	2
Total	20

Table 5.43 reveals that in case of fourteen companies, line and staff participate equally in the deliberations of budget setting. It is also observed that the deliberations, while setting budgets, are dominated by the line only in case of two companies. Analysis of data further reveals that in case of eleven companies, line and staff participate in the budget setting through formal budget committees represented by all functional directors and unit managers of the companies concerned and nine companies do not have such formal committees for budget setting. However, the budgets are finally approved by the top management in case of all the companies.

COMMUNICATION

The frequency of communication between line and staff over budget matters is summarised below in Table 5.44.

TABLE 5.44 **Line's Interaction with Staff over Budget Matters**

Level of Budget Authorities	Frequency of Interaction			
	Monthly	Quarterly	Yearly	Total
Director	-	-	16	16
Manager (G.M)	-	24	13	37
Manager	29	21	06	56
Dy. Manager	38	15	01	54
Total	67	60	36	163

Table 5.44 reveals that line managers have quite frequent interactions with the staff over budget matters. Top management is approached by line only when any serious difference of opinion arises between line and staff relating to budget matters.

RELATIONSHIPS

The relationship of line with the budget staff over budget matters in their respective organisations is summarised below in Table 5.45.

TABLE 5.45 **Cordiality of Relationship Between Line and Staff Over Budget Matters**

Degree of Relationship	Responses N	%
Very Satisfactory	12	7 %
Quite Satisfactory	15	9 %
Fairly Satisfactory	33	21 %
A Little Satisfactory	86	53 %
Very Dissatisfied	17	10 %
Total	163	100 %

Table 5.45 indicates that the relationship of line with staff is not very satisfactory in the opinion of 62 % of line managers. Only in 16 % cases, the relationship of line with staff is found satisfactory. This indicates that the relationship between line and staff over budget matters in general is not very cordial.

5.4.2 *RESPONDENTS' OPINION ABOUT PERCEIVED CHARACTERISTICS OF STAFF'S ROLE IN BUDGET SYSTEM*

The opinion of respondents' (line and staff) about the perceived characteristics of staff's role in terms of their interest, co-operation, understanding and utility of advice in the working of budget system is described as under.

INTEREST

The opinion of line and staff about staff's interest in solving the problems of line departments is summarised below in Table 5.46.

TABLE 5.46 **Interest Shown by Staff in Solving the Problems of Line Departments**

Budget Managers' interest in budgetees' problems	Response: Budget Managers N	%	Operating Managers N	%	Diff %
Always	41	43 %	24	15 %	+28 %
Mostly	19	20 %	30	18 %	+2 %
Sometimes	17	17 %	65	40 %	-23 %
Seldom	13	13 %	30	18 %	-5 %

Never	7	7 %	14	9 %	-2 %
Total	97	100 %	163	100 %	
$\bar{x}$	1.64		3.1		1.46*
S.D.	1.10		1.18		-.08

* < .01

Table 5.46 reveals that 63 % of the staff is of the opinion that they are always interested seriously in solving the problems of line managers. On the other hand, 67 % of the line managers expressed the view that the staff is not very serious about the problems of operating departments. The difference between the opinion of line and staff regarding the interest shown by staff in solving the problem of line is statistically significant at .01 level of significance.

CO-OPERATION

The opinion of line and staff about staff's co-operation with the line over budget matters is shown below in Table 5.47.

TABLE 5.47 **Staff's Co-operation with Line Over Budget Matters**

Staff's Co-operation	Response				
	Budget Managers		Operating Managers		Diff.
	N	%	N	%	%
Always	20	21 %	7	4 %	-17 %
Mostly	25	26 %	10	6 %	-20 %
Sometimes	35	36 %	34	21 %	+15 %
Seldom	8	8 %	71	44 %	-36 %
Never	9	9 %	41	25 %	-16 %
Total	97	100 %	163	100 %	
$\bar{x}$	2.60		3.72		-1.12*
S.D.	1.18		1.15		.03

* < .01

Table 5.47 indicates that 47 % of the staff are of the opinion that full co-operation is extended by them to the line in all budget matters. On the other hand, 67 % of the line managers do not corroborate the views expressed by staff regarding their co-operation in solving the problems of line. The statistical difference between the opinion of line and staff regarding staff's co-operation with line over budget matters is significant at .01 level of significance.

UNDERSTANDING

The opinion of line and staff about the staff's understanding of budgetees' problems in the larger interests of the business as a whole is presented below in Table 5.48.

TABLE 5.48 **Staff's Understanding of Budgetee's Problems**

Staff's Understanding Over Budgetees' Problems	Response				
	Budget Managers		Operating Managers		Diff.
	N	%	N	%	%
Always	55	57 %	10	6 %	51 %
Mostly	29	30 %	25	15 %	15 %
Sometimes	12	12 %	68	42 %	-30 %
Seldom	1	1 %	43	27 %	-26 %
Never	-	-	17	10 %	-10 %
Total	97	100 %	163	100 %	
$\bar{x}$	1.59		3.17		1.58*
S.D.	.76		1.03		-.27

* < .01

Table 5.48 reveals that the mean difference between the opinion of line and staff about staff's understanding of line's problems is statistically significant at .01 level of significance. It is clear from the table that in the opinion of 87 % staff, the problem of line pertaining to the attainment of budget standards is fully understood by the staff. On the other hand, 79 % of the line disagree with the opinion expressed by the staff and hold the view that specialisation of the staff is based on specialised training and experience on the subject and is not much concerned with our actual operations.

UTILITY

The views expressed by line and staff about the utility of staff's advice in the attainment of budget standards is presented below in Table 5.49.

TABLE 5.49 Utility of Staff's Advice to Line

Utility of Staff's Advice	Response				
	Staff Managers		Operating Managers		Diff.
	N	%	N	%	%
Always	65	67 %	15	9 %	+58 %
Mostly	28	29 %	24	15 %	+14 %
Sometimes	2	2 %	46	28 %	-26 %
Seldom	1	1 %	37	23 %	-22 %
Never	1	1 %	41	25 %	-24 %
Total	97	100 %	163	100 %	
$\bar{x}$	1.43		3.17		-1.74*
S.D.	.75		1.31		-.56

* < .01

Table 5.49 reveals that 96 % of the staff hold the view that their advice on budget matters is ignored by line inspite of its utility in budget matters. On the other hand, 61 % of the line are of the opinion that the staff's advice over budget matters is not very useful in attaining their budgeted performance. The statistical difference between the opinion of line and staff regarding the utility of staff's advice to line in solving their budget problems is significant at .01 level of significance.

5.4.3 *PERCEIVED ROLE OF STAFF IN BUDGET SYSTEM AND ITS IMPACT UPON LINES' JOB PERFORMANCE*

The opinion of staff about the relationship between the perceived characteristics of staff's role in budget system and its impact upon line's performance is shown below in Table 5.50.

TABLE 5.50 **Perceived Role of Staff in Budget System and its Impact Upon Line's Performance**

Staff's Role in Budget System	Line's Performance Variables			
	Influence productivity	Stimulate performance	Better work	Instructions, not budgets
Line is ignorant about the job done by my department	-.04830	-.06390	-.10013	-.01349
Staff should leave more to line	-.11206	-.03186	.15977	-.12725
Line is sufficiently cost-conscious	-.27397*	.05326	.39941*	-.04359
Service to management	.02023	.05043	-.04154	.13892

Co-operation is smooth	-.01145	-.12055	-.05042	.22917**
More co-operation is desired between line and staff	.16266	-.08454	-.03790	.00050
Line do not put in enough efforts	.15543	-.20583***	.29045*	-.01969
Line follows our advice	.17287	.07677	.18554	-.03399
Intrinsic satisfaction	.16266	.27476*	.26720*	.04188
Line is conscious for quality	.11813	.28398*	.03007	-.16699

** < .01 ** < .02 *** < .05

Table 5.50 reveals that line's job performance variables e.g. 'Budget influences line's performance'; 'Budget stimulates budgetees performance'; 'performance can be improved through budgets' are significantly correlated respectively with the variables connected with the perceived role of staff in budget system e.g. 'Line is sufficiently cost-conscious'; 'line is conscious for quality' and 'line feel satisfied when they attain their budget standards'; 'smooth cooperation between line and staff over budget matters' at .01 level of significance.

Table 5.50 further indicates that the job performance variable, viz., 'possible to work much better at reduced costs' is significantly correlated with three variables of perceived characteristics of staff's role in budget system, viz., 'Cost consciousness of line'; 'line put in enough efforts in attaining budget standards' and 'line feel satisfied with the attainment of their budget standards' - at .01 level of significance. Statistical analysis of data given in the table clearly brings out that line's cost-consciousness and their feeling of satisfaction through the attainment of budget standards are the most significant variables affecting line's performance in the opinion of staff.

The opinion of line about the relationship between perceived characteristics of staff's role in budget system and its impact upon line's performance is summarised below in Table 5.51.

TABLE 5.51: **Relationship between Perceived Role of Staff in Budget System and its Impact upon Line's Job Performance**

Staff's Role in Budget System	Job Performance Variables			
	Influence productivity	Stimulate performance	Better work	Instructions, not budgets
Staff do not take interest in the problems of line departments	0.5342	-.09546	.13733	-.12157

People from the staff deptt. lack the understanding of line department	-.08180	.10066	-.08553	.16843***
More co-operation between line and staff is desired	-.08700	.10228	-.14817	.20065*
Assistance from staff is available on budget matters	-.01941	.01290	.16318***	.02271
Line consult staff	.02105	.07129	-.05776	-.02508
Staff advice is very useful	-.01178	-.10328	-.05625	.02686

* < .01 ** < .05

Table 5.51 reveals that variables related with line's job performance e.g., possible to work much better at reduced costs'; not will improve future performance' are signifincantly correlated respectively with the variables of perceived characteristics of staff's role in budget system, e.g., 'Staff assistance is available on budget matters as and when needed'; 'more co-operation is desired between line and staff'; and 'staff fully understand Line's problems' - at .01 and .05 level of significance. This indicates that staff assistance and their co-operation with line over budget matters improve the job performance.

5.4.4 *PERCEIVED ROLE OF STAFF IN BUDGET SYSTEM AND ITS IMPACT UPON LINE'S SATISFACTION*

The opinion of staff about the relationship between perceived characteristics of staff's role in the working of budget system and its impact upon line's job satisfaction is summarised below in Table 5.52.

TABLE 5.52: **Staff's Role in Budget System and its Impact Upon Line's Job Satisfaction**

Staff's Role in Budget System	Lines' Job Satisfaction Variables			
	Like	Stress	Enjoy	Pressure
Line is ignorant about the job done by staff department	-.07715	.113564	-.08967	-.03801
Staff leaves more for line	.10513	-.01436	-.00869	-.06469
Line is insufficiently cost-conscious	-.24776**	.18640	-.14555	-.05029
Service to management	.14520	-.12114	.09710	.03282
Co-operation is smooth	.33040*	-.03030	.26753*	-.04801
Line is conscious for quality	.19424	-.17333	.23136**	.22407***
More co-operation is desired	-.05689	-.11357	-.13880	-.06332
Line does not spare enough efforts	-.13594	.15434	-.18045	.05708
Line follows our advice	.18304	-.16911	.13718	-.14946
Satisfaction through the work itself	.34134*	-.22016***	.28873*	-.08323

* < .01   ** < .02   *** < .05

Table 5.52 indicates that the line's job satisfaction variables, e.g., 'Line like the department where they work', 'Line enjoy their job', - are significantly correlated respectively with the variables of perceived role of staff in budget system, e.g., 'line derive satisfaction through the attainment of their budget standards' and 'smooth co-operation between line and staff' - at .01 level of significance. In addition to this, 'cost and quality consciousness' are also correlated with the above variables of job satisfaction at .02 level of significance. Hence, it is clear from Table 5.52 that satisfaction through work itself and smooth co-operation between line and staff are the most significant variables in providing job satisfaction to line.

The opinion of line regarding the relationship between perceived characteristics of staff's role in budget system and its impact upon line's satisfaction is summarised below in Table 5.53.

TABLE 5.53 **Staff's Role in Budget System and its Impact upon Line's Job Satis faction**

Staff's Role in Budget System	Lines' Job Satisfaction Variables Like	Nervous	Enjoy	Pressure
Staff do not take interest in the problems of line Deptt..	.08860	.01303	.04647	.00848
Lack understanding of line problems	-.02512	.06921	.04544	.00105
Co-operation between line and staff is desired	-.02512	-.00788	.09280	-.17241**
Assistance from staff is available	.19392**	-.04561	-.01462	-.06627
Staff discuss budget matters	.04328	-.02161	-.12883	-.05084
Staff advice is useful	.01872	.10385	-.04322	-.14765

** < .02

Table 5.53 shows that line's job satisfaction variables, viz., 'Line like the department where they work' and 'budgetees do not feel pressurised in their job', - are significantly correlated respectively with the variables of perceived role of staff in budget system, viz., 'availabilities of assistance of staff' and 'smooth cooperation between line and staff at .02 level of significance. This indicates that line's job satisfaction is associated with the availability of staff's assistance over budget matters as and when needed.

Analysis of data presented above in Tables 5.50 & 5.51 leads us to conclude that staff consider cost-consciousness and satisfaction through attainment of budget standards as the most significant variables in line's job performance, whereas line consider desired cooperation between line and staff as the crucial factor in line's job performance.

Analysis of data presented in Tables 5.52 and 5.53 clearly brings out that smooth co-operation between line and staff and satisfaction through work itself are the most significant factors in influencing line's job satisfaction in the opinion of the staff, whereas line consider the availability of staff assistance and desired co-operation between line and staff as the most important variables in their job satisfaction. It means that smooth co-operation between line and staff is the most crucial factor in influencing the Line's job satisfaction in the opinion of both line and staff.

5.5 EVALUATION OF BUDGET PERFORMANCE

The impact of evaluation of budget performance over the performance and job satisfaction of budgetees is described in this section. It contains four parts. Part 5.5.1 describes the various aspects of performance evaluation followed by the companies in practice. Part 5.5.2 presents the opinion of budget managers and budgetees about the perceived characteristics (refer Chapter 4, p. 75) of evaluation of budget performance. The impact of evaluation of budget performance on job performance and job satisfaction of budgetees is described in Parts 5.5.3 and 5.5.4 respectively.

5.5.1 *EVALUATION OF BUDGET PERFORMANCE IN PRACTICE*

The main aspects of budget evaluation such as key areas, participation, frequency and follow up in practice are discussed as under.

KEY AREAS OF BUDGET EVALUATION

The opinion of budgetees with regard to the importance confer to the key areas of performance by the appraisers is presented below in Table 5.54.

TABLE 5.54 **Key Areas and Importance Conferred by the Appraisers**

Areas	Maximum	Moderate	Little	No at all
Efforts	19	14	04	61
Profits	03	03	45	31
Quality	28	11	12	19
Budget	16	70	25	17
Relation with Superiors	68	17	17	05
Efficiency	17	32	28	19
Attitude towards Subordinates	02	01	10	01

Personality traits	10	15	22	10
Total	163	163	163	163

Table 5.54 indicates that 42% of the budgetees consider relation with superiors as the most critical area in the evaluation of their budget performance. Quality of the product, efforts and efficiency are ranked second, third and fourth respectively by the budgetees. Further analysis of Table 5.54 reveals that none of the budget managers interviewed could provide satisfactory basis of measuring the cost, quality and budget consciousness of their budgetees.

JOINT EVALUATION

The involvement of budgetees in the evaluation of their budgeted performance by the appraisers is summarised below in Table 5.55.

TABLE 5.55 **Involvement of Budgetees in their Performance Evaluation**

Involvement in Performance Evaluation	Response	
	Number	Percentage
Yes	43	27 %
No	120	73 %
Total	163	100 %

Table 5.55 shows that in 27 % cases, budgetees are associated in the evaluation of their budgeted performance by the appraisers. Table further reveals that 92 % of the above express that appraisers ask them to associate in the evaluation of their budgeted performance only when the variance are exceptionally significant. This indicates that performance of budgetees, in normal circumstances, is evaluated only by the appraisers such as superiors, budget managers etc.

FREQUENCY OF BUDGET EVALUATION

The areas and frequency of preparing the performance reports by the budget managers is summarised below in Table 5.56.

TABLE 5.56 **Areas and Frequency of Preparing Performance Reports**

Areas	Daily	Monthly	Quarterly	Yearly	Total
	Frequency				
Sales	-	8	11	1	20
Profit	-	3	13	4	20
Cash	18	2	-	-	20
Factory Expenses	-	-	1	19	20
Office Overheads	-	-	1	19	20
Selling and Distribution Expenses	-	3	4	13	20

Table 5.56 shows that 90 % companies prepare cash reports on daily, sales and profits reports on monthly and overhead reports on yearly basis. This indicates that performance reports are prepared by the companies in almost all the areas but more frequently in cash and sales.

FOLLOW-UP

The follow up action taken by the companies in case performance reports show significant deviations from the budget standards is summarised below in Table 5.57.

TABLE 5.57 **Follow-up Action Over Budget Variances**

Follow-up actions	Response N	%
Written explanation	67	41 %
Indication of corrective action	23	14 %
Discussion with subordinates	43	26 %
Overall explanation	30	19 %
Total	163	100 %

Table 5.57 indicates that in most of the cases of significant deviations, written explanation is demanded by the top managements from the operating managers. Oral explanation, discussion with subordinates and indication of corrective actions are also considered

equally important in case of such deviations.

5.5.2 *PERCEIVED CHARACTERISTICS OF EVALUATION OF BUDGET PERFORMANCE.*

The opinion of budget managers and budgetees about the perceived characteristics of evaluation of budget performance such as ability vs traits, self vs others and accountability of variances are described as under.

ABILITY VS TRAITS

The opinion of budget managers and budgetees about the evaluation of performance in terms of ability vs traits is summarised below in Table 5.58.

TABLE 5.58 **Opinion of Budget Managers and Budgetees Over Evaluation of Budget Performance in Terms of Ability vs Traits**

Evaluation on ability basis	Response Budget Managers		Budgetees		Difference
	N	%	N	%	%
Always	30	31 %	03	2 %	+29 %
Mostly	39	41 %	13	8 %	+33 %
Sometimes	18	18 %	23	14 %	+4 %
Seldom	8	8 %	77	48 %	-40 %
Never	2	2 %	47	28 %	-26 %
Total	97	100 %	163	100 %	
$\bar{x}$	2.13		3.79		1.66*
S. D.	1.04		1.98		-.94

* < .01

Table 5.58 shows that 75 % of the operating managers express that their performance is evaluated by the appraisers on the basis of personal traits rather than ability to attain standards. On the other hand, 72 % of the budget managers interviewed are of the opinion that the performance of the budgetees is evaluated on the basis of their ability to attain standards rather than traits. The difference between the opinion of budget managers and budgetees pertaining to the evaluation of their budget performance is statistically significant at .01 level of significance.

SELF VS OTHERS

The opinion of budget managers and budgetees about budgetees' involvement in the evaluation of their budget performance is presented below in Table 5.59.

TABLE 5.59 **Opinion of Budget Managers and Budgetees About the Involvemen: of Budgetees in the Evaluation of their Budget Performance.**

Self Evaluation	Response Budget Managers		Budgetees		Difference
	N	%	N	%	%
Always	48	50 %	10	6 %	+44 %
Mostly	43	44 %	25	15 %	+29 %
Sometimes	4	4 %	32	18 %	-14 %
Seldom	2	2 %	49	31	-29 %
Never	-	-	47	30	-30 %
Total	97	100 %	163	100 %	
$\overline{x}$	1.63		3.61		-1.98
S.D.	.75		1.23		-.48

* < . 01

Table 5.59 reveals that 94 % of the budget managers express that budgetees are given due opportunity to evaluate their performance with their appraisers. On the other hand, 79 % of the budgetees do not corroborate the opinion expressed by budget managers and state that they are informed by the appraisers only when the deviations are exceptionally high. The difference between the opinion of budgetees and budget managers over involvement of budgetees in the evaluation of their budget performance is statistically significant at .01 level of significance.

ACCOUNTABILITY

Table 5.60 presents below the opinion of budget managers and budgetees regarding the budgetees, accountability to their budget variances.

TABLE 5.60 **Budgetees' Accountability to Budget Variances**

Budgetees' Accountability	Response Budget Managers N	%	Budgetees N	%	Difference %
Always	30	31 %	65	40 %	-9 %
Mostly	33	34 %	60	37 %	-03 %
Sometimes	26	27 %	23	14 %	+ 13 %
Seldom	4	4 %	8	5 %	-1 %
Never	4	4 %	7	4 %	+6 %
Total	97	100 %	163	100 %	
$\bar{x}$	2.28		1.98		-.30ns
S.D.	1.25		1.04		.21

ns : not significant

Table 5.60 reveals that 65 % of the budget managers hold the view that budgetees are personally held accountable for their budget variances. On the other hand, 77 % of the budgetees also hold the same opinion as expressed by budget managers. The difference between the opinion of budget managers and budgetees about the budgetees' accountability to their budget variances is not significant even at .05 level of significance and hence they are held personally accountable for variances.

5.5.3 *BUDGET EVALUATION AND BUDGETEES' JOB PERFORMANCE*

The opinion of budget managers about the relationship between perceived characteristics of budget evaluation and its impact upon budgetees' job performance is presented below in Table 5.61.

TABLE 5.61 **Opinion of Budget Managers about the Relationship Between Performance Evaluation and Budgetees Job Performance**

Performance evaluation variables	Influence Productivity	Performance Variables Stimulate Performance	At reduced costs	Instructions, not budgets
Ability to attain standards	-.04153	-.21565***	-.04490	-.03357
Yardsticks	.01053	.20190***	.03031	.04839
Accountability	.00707	-.04644	-.01879	-.02537

Negative variances	.09450	-.06569	.10664	.21659***
Physical targets	-.17624	.10936	.15846	.03401
Self Evaluation	-.12146	.22652*	.18849	-.31602*
Pay/Promotion	-.7917	.12172	.14811	.03903

* <.01   ** < .02   *** < .05

Table 5.61 indicates that the variables of budgetees job performance - 'budget stimulates budgetees performance' and 'budget, not instructions will improve future performance' are significantly correlated with the variable of performance evaluation - 'self evaluation' - at .01 level of significance. It indicates that self evaluation is the most significant variable in stimulating the budgetees for better job performance.

The opinion of budgetees about the perceived characteristics of performance evaluation and its impact upon their performance is summarised below in Table 5.62.

TABLE 5.62 **The Opinion of Budgetees About the Relationship Between Performance Evaluation and Budgetees Job Performance**

Performance Evaluation Variables	Performance Evaluation Variables Influence Productivity	Stimulate Performance	At reduced costs	Instructions, not budgets
Ability to attain stdandards	.11474	-.05142	.11852	-.08184
Accountability	.11536	.04710	-.02480	-.07599
Self evaluation	.16503***	-.04782	.04438	.05246
Human costs	-.13056	-.01459	-.01958	.05933
Explanation	.07684	-.13504	.02429	-.00647

* < .01   ** < .02   *** < .05

Table 5.62 reveals that variable of performance evaluation - 'self evaluation' - is significantly correlated with the variable of budgetees' job performance - 'budget stimulates better performance' - at .05 level of significance. This leads to conclude that self evaluation is the most significant variable of performance evaluation in stimulating the budgetees for better performance in the opinion of both budgetees and budget managers.

5.5.4 PERFORMANCE EVALUATION AND BUDGETEES' JOB SATISFACTION

On the other hand, the opinion of budget managers about the relationship between the perceived characteristics of performance evaluation and budgetees job satisfaction is shown below in Table 5.63.

TABLE 5.63 **The Opinion of Budget Managers About the Relationship Between Performance Evaluation and Budgetees Job Satisfaction**

Performance Evaluation Variables	Job Satisfaction Variables			
	Like	Tension	Enjoy	Pressure
Ability to attain standards	.05953	-.11462	.22697**	-.20837***
Yardstick	.17936	.02107	.03654	-.18154
Accountability	.10459	-.02324	.11011	-.05741
Variances	.18277	-.02180	.22882**	-.13337
Physical Standards	.16281	.02516	.04364	-.18899
Self Evaluation	.18230	-.05251	.15688	.00744
Pay/Promotion	-.01486	-.07236	.08740	-.11308

** < .02 *** < .05

Table 5.63 indicates that the variables of performance evaluation - 'ability to attain budget standards' and 'expressing satisfaction over variances' - are significantly correlated with the variable of job satisfaction - 'budgetees enjoy their job' - at .02 level of significance. Analysis of data further confirm that ability rather trait and appreciation rather criticism of budget evaluation are better source of budgetee's satisfaction.

The opinion of budgetees about the relationship between variables of budget evaluation and its impact upon budgetees job satisfaction is presented below in Table 5.64.

TABLE 5.64 **The Opinion of Budgetees About the Relationship Between Performance Evaluation and its Impact upon their Job Satisfaction**

Performance Evaluation Variables	Job Satisfaction Variables			
	Like	Tension	Enjoy	Pressure
Ability to attain standards	.03663	.08153	.30433*	-.200220*
Accountability	.08303	-.10697	.06969	-.17407
Self Evaluation	-.07590	.00037	.093991	.11726
Human Costs	.01311	.01302	-.07476	.05929
Explanation	-.11294	-.00742	-.03912	-.00681

* < .01

Table 5.64 reveals that the performance evaluation variable - 'evaluation of ability to attain budget standards' - is significantly correlated with the job satisfaction variables - 'budgetees enjoy their jobs' and 'absence of pressure' - at .01 level of significance. This indicates that budgetees get more satisfaction when their ability to perform rather personality traits are made the criteria of evaluation of their budgeted performance.

This leads us to conclude that budgetees ability to attain budget standards is the most significant variable in providing job satisfaction to budgetees in the opinion of both budget managers and budgetees.

5.6 FEEDBACK OF PERFORMANCE EVALUATION

The impact of feedback of performance evaluation on the job performance and job satisfaction of budgetees is described in this section. It contains four parts. Part 5.6.1 is devoted to the practice of feedback of performance evaluation followed by the companies in the sample for study. Part 5.6.2 presents the opinion of budget managers and budgetees about the perceived characteristics of feedback (refer to Chapter 4, p.75). and finally, the impact of perceived characteristics of feedback on the job performance and job satisfaction of budgetees is discussed in Parts 5.6.3 and 5.6.4 respectively.

5.6.1 *FEEDBACK PRACTICES IN SAMPLE COMPANIES*

The practice of feedback followed by the companies in the

sample in terms of preparation, frequency, channel, coverage, uses, characteristics and follow-up of performance reports is described hereunder:

PREPARATION

The practice of preparation of performance reports followed by the companies in the sample is summarised below in Table 5.65.

TABLE 5.65 **Preparation of Performance Reports**

Preparation of Performance Reports	Response	
	N	%
Yes	20	100 %
No	-	-
Total	20	100 %

Table 5.65 indicates that the performance reports (i.e., variance reports) are prepared by all the companies in the sample. It means that the companies consider performance reports as an important instrument of controlling the overall performance of budgetees in the companies concerned.

FREQUENCY

The frequency of performance reports by the companies is presented below in Table 5.66.

TABLE 5.66 **Frequency of Performance Reports**

Periodicity	Response	
	N	%
Monthly	9	45 %
Quarterly	8	40 %
Half-yearly	2	10 %
Yearly	1	5 %
Total	20	100 %

Table 5.66 indicates that performance reports are prepared on monthly, quarterly, half-yearly and yearly basis by nine, eight, two

and one companies respectively. It indicates that most of the companies (85 %) in the sample prepare their performance reports on monthly and quarterly basis.

CHANNEL

The various channels of communicating the performance results to the budgetees are shown below in Table 5.67.

TABLE 5.67 **Channel of Communicating the Performance Results to Budgetees**

Channel of Communication	Response	
	N	%
Immediate Supervisor	121	75 %
Budget Manager	32	19 %
Others	10	6 %
Total	163	100 %

Table 5.67 reveals that budgetees are informed about their performance results by their immediate supervisors in 75 % cases and by the budget managers in 19 % cases. Only in 4 % cases, budgetees are informed about their performance by people other than immediate supervisors and budget managers.

COVERAGE

The coverage of performance reports communicated to the budgetees is presented below in Table 5.68.

TABLE 5.68 **Conveyance of Performance Reports Communicated to Budgetees**

Coverage of results	Response	
	N	%
Failure	113	69 %
Success	16	10 %
Both	34	21 %
Total	163	100 %

Table 5.68 shows that in 69% cases, budgetees are informed about their failures only. In 21% cases, both failures and successes

are reported to them through performance reports. This indicates that the coverage of performance reports is dominated by failures of budgetees rather than successes.

USES

The uses of performance reports sent to the budgetees are presented below in Table 5.69.

TABLE 5.69 **Use of Performance Results**

Uses of Results	Response	
	N	%
Next Budget	68	41 %
Warning	25	14 %
Formality	43	27 %
None	27	18 %
Total	163	100 %

Table 5.69 reveals that in 41 % cases, performance reports are used as a basis to develop the next year's budgets of the companies, whereas in 45 % cases, these reports are prepared for the sake of formality which indicates that performance reports are not fully utilised in improving the performance of budgetees in their respective organisations.

CHARACTERISTICS

The characteristics of performance reports communicated to the budgetees is shown below in Table 5.70.

TABLE 5.70 **Characteristics of Performance Reports**

Characteristics of Performance Reports	Response			
	Relevant	Clear	Useful	Type of Reports
Cumbersome	79 %	34 %	63 %	59 %
Simple	21 %	66 %	37 %	41 %
Total	100 %	100 %	100 %	100 %

Table 5.70 indicates that in the opinion of 59 % budgetees the performance reports are found to be cumbersome. However, further analysis of the table reveals that cumbersome reports are found to be more relevant (79 %) and useful (63 %) as compared to the simple reports. But simple reports are found to be more clear in the opinion of budgetees as compared to cumbersome reports.

FOLLOW-UP

The follow-up of performance reports is summarised below in Table 5.71.

TABLE 5.71 **Follow-up of Performance Reports**

Follow-up	Response	
	N	%
No follow-up	61	37 %
Occasional follow-up	53	33 %
Frequent follow-up	27	17 %
Systematic follow-up	22	13 %
Total	163	100 %

Table 5.71 indicates that follow-up actions are taken only in 63 % cases. Further analysis of the responses reveals that systematic and frequent follow-up actions are taken only in 13 % and 17 % cases respectively.

5.6.2 *PERCEIVED CHARACTERISTICS OF FEEDBACK*

The opinion of budget managers and budgetees about the perceived characteristics of feedback of performance results in terms of reporting, frequency and specificity is described as under.

FEEDBACK OF PERFORMANCE EVALUATION

The opinion of budget managers and budgetees about the feedback of performance results to the budgetees by the appraisers is presented below in Table 5.72.

TABLE 5.72 **Reporting of Performance Evaluation to Budgetees**

Reporting of Performance Evaluation	Response				
	Budget Managers		Operating Managers		Diff.
	N	%	N	%	%
Always	16	16 %	8	5 %	+11 %
Mostly	23	24 %	25	15 %	+9 %
Sometimes	10	10 %	20	12 %	-2 %
Seldom	23	24 %	52	32 %	-8 %
Never	25	26 %	58	36 %	-10 %
Total	**97**	**100 %**	**163**	**100 %**	
$\bar{x}$	3.05		3.75		-.70 ns
S.D.	1.42		1.09		+.33

ns: not significant

Table 5.72 indicates that the statistical difference between the opinion of budget managers and budgetees pertaining to reporting of performance evaluation to the budgetees by the appraisers is insignificant even at .05 level of significance. It means that the performance reports are made available to the budgetees by the appraisers in the opinion of both budget managers and the budgetees.

SPECIFICITY OF FEEDBACK OF PERFORMANCE EVALUATION

The opinion of budget managers and budgetees with regard to the specificity of feedback of performance reports is shown below in Table 5.73.

TABLE 5.73 **Specificity in Reporting of Performance Evaluation**

Specificity in Reporting Performance Evaluation	Response				
	Budget Managers		Operating Managers		Diff. in
	N	%	N	%	%
Always	28	29 %	8	5 %	+24 %
Mostly	35	36 %	8	5 %	+31 %
Sometimes	28	29 %	18	11 %	+18 %
Seldom	06	6 %	76	47 %	-41 %
Never	-	-	53	33 %	-33 %
Total	97	**100 %**	**163**	**100 %**	
$\bar{x}$	2.14		4.03		-1.89*
S.D.	.92		1.04		-.12

* < .01

Table 5.73 indicates that 65 % of budget managers hold the view that the performance reports in specific form, are made available to the budgetees. On the other hand, budgetees do not corroborate the opinion of budget managers and state that the feedback of performance evaluation is general and not very specific in terms of their actions, responsibility, area of operations and controllability aspects of their performance. The difference between the opinion of budget managers and budgetees about the specificity of feedback of performance evaluation to the budgetees is statistically significant at .01 level of significance.

FREQUENCY OF FEEDBACK OF PERFORMANCE EVALUATION

The opinion of budget managers and budgetees about the frequency of feedback of performance evaluation to the budgetees is presented below in Table 5.74.

TABLE 5.74 **Frequency of Reporting Performance Evaluation**

Frequency	Response				
	Budget Manager		Operating Managers		Diff.
	N	%	N	%	%
Always	22	22 %	8	5 %	+17 %
Mostly	46	48 %	25	15 %	+33 %
Sometimes	26	27 %	20	12 %	+15 %
Seldom	1	1 %	52	32 %	-31 %
Never	2	2 %	58	36 %	-34 %
Total	97	100 %	163	100 %	
$\bar{x}$	2.12		3.75		-1.63*
S.D.	.84		1.09		-.25

* < .01

Table 5.74 indicates that in the opinion of 70% of budget managers performance reports are communicated to the budgetees without delay. On the other hand, 68% of the operating managers do not agree with the opinion expressed by the budget managers and state that performance reports are not made available to them frequently and in time. The difference between the opinion of budget managers and budgetees pertaining to the frequency of budget evaluation to the budgetees is significant at .01 level of significance.

5.6.3 *FEEDBACK OF PERFORMANCE EVALUATION AND JOB PERFORMANCE AND JOB SATISFACTION*

The opinion of budget managers about the relationship between the perceived characteristics of feedback of Performance Evaluation and its impact upon budgetees job performance is shown below in Table 5.75.

TABLE 5.75 **Feedback of Performance Evaluation And Budgetees Job Performance**

Feedback Variables	Budgetee's Job Performance variables			
	Influence Productivity	Stimulate Performance	Reduced cost	Instructions, not budgets
Reporting of failures	.27976*	.06806	.17263	.14978
Action of line managers	.32726*	.27715*	.11060	.25756*
Controllable aspects	.19442	.32647*	.31303*	.06819
Within responsibility	.20809***	.18190	-.00285	.06004
Measurable areas	.35079*	.17579	.11700	.00323
Participation in feedback	.25368*	.30679*	.27885*	.05755

* < .01 *** < .05

Table 5.75 indicates that the variables of feedback of Performance Evaluation - 'actions of line mangers' and 'participation in feedback' - are significantly correlated with the variables of budgetees' job performance - 'influences productivity', 'stimulates performance' and 'works better at reduced costs' - at .01 level of significance. Further analysis of data reveals that the feedback of Performace Evaluation variables - 'reporting of failures', 'controllable aspects' and 'measurable areas' - are also significantly correlated at .01 level of significance with the variables of budgetees' job performance 'influences Productivity', 'Stimulates Performance', and 'work better at reduced costs' - at .01 level of significance. It leads us to conclude that budgetees participation in the feedback sessions and feedback on their operations are most crucial factors in influencing the budgetees' job performance in the opinion of budget managers.

The opinion of budget managers about the relationship between the perceived characteristics of feedback of Performance Evaluation and its impact upon budgetees job satisfaction is summarised below in Table 5.76.

TABLE 5.76 **Relationship Between Feedback and Budgetees Job Satisfaction**

Feedback Variables	Job Satisfaction of Variables			
	Like	Tension	Enjoy	Pressure
Reporting of failures	.01675	-.12175	.23388**	.01800
Actions of line managers	.15483	-.10834	.16585	-.15590
Controllable aspects	.20528***	-.14103	.26024*	-.14385
Within responsibility	.01842	-.30399*	.12789	.00725
Measurable areas	.06109	-.19823	.22253**	-.25316*
Participation in feedback	.12085	.03039	.10402	-.24789**

* < .01 ** < .02 *** < .05

Table 5.76 indicates that the variables of budgetee's job satisfaction- 'Budgets do not make budgetees agitated and nervous', 'budgetees enjoy their jobs' and 'budgetees are under pressure on their jobs' - are significantly correlated with the variables of feedback of performance evaluation - 'reporting matters relevant to budgetee's responsibility' , 'reporting controllable and measurable aspects of performance' - at .01 level of significance respectively. This indicates that if performance evaluation is within the controllable limits, budgetees enjoy their job with such reportings. Further analysis of Table 5.76 clearly brings out that, in the opinion of budget managers, reporting within the responsible and measurable areas of performance reduces budgetees tensions, nervousness and pressure on their jobs and hence improve their job satisfaction.

5.6.4 *FEEDBACK OF PERFORMANCE EVALUATION AND JOB SATISFACTION AND JOB PERFORMANCE*

The opinion of budgetees about the relationship between the perceived characteristics of feedback of Performance Evaluation and its impact upon their job performance is summarised below in Table

5.77.

TABLE 5.77 **Feedback of Performance Evaluation and Budgetee's Job Performance**

Feedback Variables	Variables of Job Performance			
	Influences Productivity	Stimulates Performance	Reduced costs	Instructions, not budgets
Sufficiently understandable	.19687*	-.08485	-.04979	-.09780
Convey attainments	.00694	-.00844	-.01141	-.13772
Shown without delay	.07763	-.15659***	.03533	-.04050
Telling of Evaluation	.04266	-.12449	-.01025	.01774
Free and frank dialogue	.10635	.03294	.00175	.07339
Free flow of information	.00890	.03622	.06699	-.09143

* < .01 *** < .05

Analysis of data shown in Table 5.77 reveals that the variables of budgetees' job performance - 'Budget influence budgetees performance' and 'budget stimulates budgetees for better performance' - are significantly correlated with the variables of feedback of Performance evaluation - 'Evaluation reports are sufficiently understandable; and are 'shown to budgetees without delay' - at .01 level of significance respectively. This indicates that sufficiently understandable reports influence and stimulate the budgetees in improving their budgeted performance.

Table 5.78 presents below the opinion of budgetees about the relationship between the perceived characteristics of feedback of Performance Evaluation and its impact on their job satisfaction.

TABLE 5.78 **Feedback of Performance Evaluation and Budgetee's Job Satisfaction**

Feedback Variables	Job Satisfaction Variables			
	Like	Tension	Enjoy	Pressure
Sufficiently understandable	.19687**	-.08485	-.04979	-.07980
Attainments	.00694	-.00844	-.01141	+.13772

Shown without delay	.07763	-.15699***	-.03533	-.04050
Considerable information	.04266	-.12449	.01025	.01774
Free and frank dialogue	.10635	.03294	-.00125	.071339
Free flow of Information	.00890	.03622	.00699	-.09144

** < . 02 *** < .05

Table 5.78 reveals that the variables of job satisfaction - 'budgetees like the department where they work' and 'budget makes budgetees agitated and nervous' - is significantly correlated with the variables of feedback - 'sufficiently understandable' and 'timely reports' - at .02 and .05 level of significance. This indicates that clear and timely performance evaluation reports are found to be important variables in improving the job satisfaction of budgetees.

6

DEMOGRAPHIC VARIABLES

This chapter describes the demographic variables - age, education, experience, status, personality and culture - of budget managers and budgetees and impact of each variable upon their attitude towards the budget system, budgetees' job performance and job satisfaction. Section 6.1 is devoted to the mean differences between the demographic characteristics of budgetees and budget managers. Section 6.2 describes the impact of demographic characteristics of budget managers and budgetees on their attitude towards budget system. Section 6.3 and 6.4 are devoted to the relationship between demographic variables of respondents (budget managers and budgetees) and budgetees' job performance and job satisfaction respectively.

6.1 DEMOGRAPHIC CHARACTERISTICS OF RESPONDENTS

The demographic characteristics of budgetees and budget managers and the mean difference thereof are summarised below in Table 6.1.

Table 6.1 reveal that the difference between demographic variable - Status - of the budget managers and budgetees in the company concerned is only statistically significant at .01 level of significance. The difference between other demographic variables of budget managers and operating managers are insignificant. This indicates that the status of budget managers is better as compared to budgetees in the companies concerned.

TABLE 6.1 **Mean Differences of Demographic Variables of B.M. and O.M.**

Demographic Characteristics	Response (Mean Values) Staff	Line	Differences
Age	2.88	2.44	+.44
Education	2.60	2.52	+.08
Experience (total)	1.97	2.18	-.21
Experience (Budgets)	1.93	1.57	+.36
Status	4.23	2.52	+1.71*
Working comes naturally to most people	2.27	2.41	-.14
A clear order is better than consultation	2.12	2.81	-.69
Department demands my utmost effort	2.62	1.97	+.65
Obedience and respect are important virtues children should learn	1.75	1.66	+.09
People are less willing to carry responsibility then they used to be	2.78	2.74	+.04
Young people sometimes turn rebellious but settle down as they grow mature	2.57	1.90	+.67
Subordinates ought to accept superior's orders without reservation	2.46	2.24	+.24

N.B.: B.M. = Budget Managers O.M. = Operating Managers (Budgetees)
* < .01

6.2 DEMOGRAPHIC CHARACTERISTICS OF RESPONDENTS AND ITS IMPACT UPON THEIR ATTITUDE TOWARDS BUDGET SYSTEM

The opinion of budget managers about the impact of demographic variables upon their attitude towards budget system is shown below in Table 6.2.

TABLE 6.2 **Demographic Variables of Budget Managers and its Impact upon their Attitude Towards Budget System**

Demographic Variables of Budget Managers	Attitude towards budget system			
	Accounting Tool	Game to Play	Worth More	Improve Efficiency
Age	-.052	-.174	.058	-.130
Education	-.324	.014	.150	-.028
Experience (total)	.006	.036	.286	-.104
Experience (Budget)	-.001	-.178	.101	-.118
Status	.013	.111	.063	.170
Working comes naturally to most people	.367*	.165	.171	.314
Clear order is better than consultation	.156	.062	.038	.176
Obedience and respect are important virtues	.310*	.081	.066	.232*
People are less willing to work	.077	-.168	.281*	.049
Young people settle down as they become mature	.026	-.085	.029	.232*
Subordinates should obey superiors	.237**	-.047	-.005	.365*

* < .01 ** < .02

Table 6.2 indicates that the demographic variables of budget managers- 'low education', 'working comes naturally to most people', and 'obedience and respect are important virtues children should learn' - are significantly correlated with the variables of budget system - 'budget is an accounting tool' - at .01 level of significance. On the other hand, none of the demographic variables of budget managers are significantly correlated with the variable of game aspect of budget system - 'Budget is a game to play' - even at .05 level of significance. This indicates that budget managers with low education, who believe in submissiveness and are ignorant about the learning aspect of life, consider budgeting as a tool of accounting control rather than a potential tool of motivation for budgetees.

Analysis of data given in Table 6.2 further reveals that the variables of budget system - 'budget costs more than they are worth'; 'budget improves budgetees' performance' - are significantly correlated with the demographic variables of budget managers - 'association with company'; and 'people are less willing to carry responsibility than they used to be'; 'Working comes naturally to most people', and 'subordinates ought to accept superior's decisions without reservation' - at .01 level of significance respectively. This means that budget managers consider budgeting as an important tool which is worth more than the cost incurred on it. However, budget becomes costly in the opinion of budget managers when budgetees are lazy and not willing to co-operate with them on budget matters. It is also observed that budget managers consider budgeting as an important tool to improve the efficiency of budgetees provided the budgetees themselves believe in the culture of accepting the superior's decisions without reservation.

The opinion of budgetees about the impact of demographic variables upon their attitude towards budget system is presented below in Table 6.3.

TABLE 6.3 **Demographic Variables of Budgetees and its Impact upon their Attitude towards Budget System**

Demographic Variables	Variables of budget system			
	Accounting Tool	Game to Play	Worth More	Improve Efficiency
Age	-.027	.033	-.012	-.012
Education	-.077	-.031	.027	.115
Experience (total)	.047	-.085	-.054	-.063
Experience (budget)	-.055	.063	-.005	-.063
Status	-.105	.035	.043	.001
Working is natural	.057	-.051	.174**	.141
Clear order is better	-.031	.152***	.020	-.024
Plant demands my utmost efforts	.054	-.135	.151***	.118
Obedience and respect are important virtues	-.080	-.117	.080	.031
People are less willing to work	.167***	.050	-.117	-.136
Young people settle down as they become mature	.061	-.258*	.157***	-.047
Subordinates ought to accept superiors decisions	.184	.123	.001	.123

* <.01 ** < .02 *** < .05

Table 6.3 reveals that the variable of budget system - 'job is heavier with standards' - is significantly correlated with the demographic variable of budgetees - 'Young people sometimes get rebellious but settle down as they grow mature'- at .01 level of significance. It means that budgetees initially feel under pressure on the job with budgets, but this attitude of budgetees changes and they start preferring to work with budgets as they become mature.

6.3 DEMOGRAPHIC CHARACTERISTICS AND BUDGETEE'S JOB PERFORMANCE

The opinion of budget managers about the impact of demographic variables upon the budgetee's job performance is shown below in Table 6.4.

TABLE 6.4 **Demographic Characteristics of Budget Managers and their Perception about Budgetee's Job Performance**

Demographic Variables	Performance Variables			
	Influence Productivity	Stimulate Performance	Work at reduced costs	Instructions, not budgets
Age	-.172	-.353*	-.172	.147
Education	.001	.103	-.131	-.107
Experience (Total)	-.205***	-.168	-.222***	.118
Experience (Budgets)	-.042	-.246**	.133	.159
Status	.037	-.001	.079	-.008
Working is natural	.015	.188	.117	-.117
Clear order is better	.180	.105	-.022	.249*
Department demands my utmost efforts	.000	-.196	-.086	.134
Obedience and respect are important virtues	-.072	.112	-.104	.057
People are less willing to work	-.271*	-.202***	-.209***	.215***
Young people settle down as they grow mature	-.076	-.065	.039	.147
Subordinate should accept superior's decisions	.185	.124	.002	.123

* < .01 ** < .02 *** < .05

Table 6.4 reveals that the performance variables of budgetees - 'budgets influence budgetee's performance'; 'budgets stimulate budgetees for better performance'; and 'instructions, not budgets will improve future performance' - are significantly correlated with the demographic variables of budget managers - 'people are willing to work'; 'lower age group'; and 'clear order is better than consultation' - at .01 level of significance respectively. This indicates that budgets not only influence but also stimulate budgetees who belong to lower age group and are willing to work through budgets for better performance in the opinion of budget managers.

Table 6.5 presents below the opinion of budgetees about the impact of demographic variables upon job performance.

TABLE 6.5 **Demographic Variables of Budgetees and their Job Performance**

Demographic Variables	Performance Variables: Influence Productivity	Stimulate Performance	Work at reduced costs	Instructions, not budgets
Age	-.086	-.105	.705	-.023
Education	.012	.026	-.091	.074
Experience (Total)	.057	.026	-.096	.063
Experience (Budget)	.116	.167***	-.015	.053
Status	-.045	-.022	.073	.063
Work is natural	-.079	.013	.068	.018
Clear order is better	-.074	.074	-.123	-.029
Department demands my utmost efforts	.045	.064	.119	-.018
Obedience and respect are important virtues	.013	.197*	.022	-.128
People are less willing to work	.105	-.053	-.005	-.128
Young people turn rebellious but settle down as they grow mature	.097	-.006	.027	-.039
Subordinates ought to accept superior's decisions	.216*	.097	-.126	.072

* < .01 *** < .05

Table 6.5 reveals that the variables of the budgetees' job performance - 'Budgets influence budgetees' performance', and 'budgets stimulate budgetees for better performance' - are significantly correlated with the demographic variables of budgetees - 'Subordinates ought to accept superior's orders without reservation', and 'obedience and respect are important virtues children should learn' - at .01 level of significance. This indicates that budgetees who believe in the culture of obedience and respect for elders improve their performance at reduced costs.

6.4 DEMOGRAPHIC VARIABLES AND BUDGETEE'S JOB SATISFACTION

The opinion of budget managers about the impact of demographic variables upon the budgetee's job satisfaction is summarised below in Table 6.6.

TABLE 6.6 **Demographic Variables of Budget Managers and its Impact Upon Their Perception about Budgetee's Job Satisfaction.**

Demographic Variables	Job Satisfaction Variables			
	Like the Department	Tension	Enjoy the Job	Pressure
Age	-.144	.009	-.193	-.107
Education	.099	.016	.057	.114
Experience (Total)	-.026	-.010	-.104	.234**
Experience (Budgets)	-.229**	-.033	-.170	.274*
Status	.009	.032	.179	-.099
Working is natural	.437*	-.227**	.356*	-.208***
A clear order is better	.048	-.184	.109	.152
Department demands my utmost efforts	-.013	.089	.044	.014
Respect for elders	.360*	-.247**	.268*	-.065
People are less willing to work	-.093	.295*	-.158	.273*
Young people settle down as they grow mature	.098	.120	.127	-.124
Subordinates ought to accept superior's decisions without reservation	.265*	-.055	.201***	-.153

* <. 01 ** < .02 and *** < .05

Table 6.6 indicates that job satisfaction variables of budgetees - 'budgetees like the department where they work'; and 'budgetees enjoy their jobs through budgets' - are significantly correlated with the demographic variables of budget managers - 'working comes naturally to most people', 'obedience and respect are important virtues children should learn', and 'subordinates ought to accept decisions of their superiors without reservation' - at .01 level of significance. This indicates that the liking for the department and job satisfaction of budgetees largely depend upon their self-involvement in budget system and belief in the culture of obedience and respect of elders, in the opinion of budget managers.

It is further observed that job dissatisfaction variables of budgetees - 'budgetees feel agitated and nervous' and 'budgetees feel under pressure' - are significantly correlated with the demographic variables of budget managers - 'people are less willing to work'; and 'longer experience with budgetees' - at .01 level of significance. This indicates that unwillingness of budgetees to carry their responsibility and longer experience with budget system put budgetees under pressure on the job and consequently made them agitated and nervous.

The opinion of budgetees about the impact of demographic variables upon their job satisfaction is described below in Table 6.7.

TABLE 6.7 **Demographic Variables of Budgetees and its Impact upon their Job Satisfaction**

Demographic	Job Satisfaction Variables			
Variables	Like	Tension	Enjoy	Pressure
Age	-.069	-.114	-.003	.013
Education	-.068	.007	-.050	.094
Experience (Total)	-.103	-.123	.017	-.126
Experience (Budgets)	-.133	-.002	.032	.034
Status	.065	.021	.043	.207*
Working is natural	.162***	-.057	.098	-.039
Clear order is better	-.001	-.023	-.070	.129
Plant demands my utmost efforts	.115	.053	.101	-.021
Respect of elders is an important virtue	.236*	-.129	.089	-.150***
People are less willing to work	.105	.173***	.054	.007
Young people settle down as they grow mature	.050	-.008	.085	.006
Subordinates ought to accept senior's decisions	.192**	-.147	.137	.129

* < .01 ** < .02 *** < .05

Table 6.7 reveals that the variables of budgetees' job satisfaction-'budgetees like the department where they work', and 'budgets put budgetees under pressure on the job' - are significantly correlated with demographic variables of budgetees - 'obedience and respect are important virtues children should learn'; and 'higher status' - at .01 level of significance. This indicates that budgets improve the budgetees' liking for the department where they work when they believe in the culture of respect and obedience of elders. However, they feel under pressure in their jobs when they are promoted to higher positions in the organisation carrying heavier responsibilities.

7

CORPORATE CHARACTERISTICS

The impact of organisational characteristics on the attitude, performance and job satisfaction of budgetees is described in this chapter. Section 7.1 has been devoted to the organisational characteristics of the companies in the sample. Section 7.2 presents the relationship between organisational characteristics and attitude of respondents towards budget system, and finally, the relationships between organisational characteristics and job satisfaction and job performance of budgetees are described in Sections 7.3 and 7.4 respectively.

7.1 ORGANISATIONAL CHARACTERISTICS OF THE COMPANIES

The organisational characteristics of the companies in the sample are summarised below in Table 7.1.

Table 7.1 indicates that the study covers both - Private and Public sector manufacturing companies having turnover ranging from Rs. 25 crores to Rs. 3000 crores and strength of employees from 1200 to 2,00,000. It is observed that of the companies, 16 have product leadership in the national markets. 55% of the companies are operating in the single or similar lines of products and 30% have diversified lines of operation. Further analysis of the table reveals that 55% of the companies consider their technology as one of the best in India, and the rest are above average (25%) and average (20%) respectively. Most of the companies have a considerable degree of decentralisation in their decision-making process.

TABLE 7.1 **Corporate Characteristics of the Sample Companies**

	Employees (N)	Turnover (in crores)	Market Dominance	Complexity	Technology	Autonomy of Operations
Pvt-1	9000	250	National	Diversified	One of the best	Substantial
2	13000	196	National	Diversified	One of the best	Substantial
3	16000	250	National	Related	One of the best	Substantial
4	6000	150	None	Diversified	Average	Substantial
5	4600	400	International	Diversified	Best	Full
6	1500	25	National	Single	Above Average	Full
7	1200	80	National	Diversified	Best	Substantial
8	3000	1300	International	Diversified	Above Average	Full
9	1582	120	International	Single	Above Average	Full
10	9000	50	National	Single	Average	Full
Pbl-1	6000	200	National	Single	Best	Substantial
2	4524	370	National	Single	Best	Substantial
3	200000	3000	National	Single	Best	Full
4	13800	247	National	Related	Best	Substantial
5	72000	1302	National	Related	Best	Full
6	15000	1338	National	Single	Best	Full
7	3000	40	National	Single	Average	Substantial
8	11000	1100	National	Single	Average	Substantial
9	6500	106	National	Single	Above Average	Substantial
10	6000	400	National	Single	Above Average	Substantial

7.2 ORGANISATIONAL CHARACTERISTICS AND RESPONDENT'S ATTITUDE TOWARDS BUDGET SYSTEM

The opinion of budgetees about the relationship between the organisational characteristics and their attitude towards budget system is summarised below in Table 7.2.

Table 7.2 will reveal that none of the variables of organisational characteristics are significantly correlated with the variables of budgetees attitude towards budget system even at .05 level of significance.

TABLE 7.2 **Organisational Characteristics and Respondent's Attitude Towards Budget System**

Organisational Characteristics	Attitude Towards Budget System Variables			
	Accounting Control	Game to Play	Job Heavier without standards	Prefer to work
Size	.057	.116	.085	.061
Market	.050	-.157	-.002	.130
Diversified	.148	.016	-.026	.033
Technology	.137	.103	-.072	-.010
Autonomy	.037	.004	.012	.100

Table 7.3 given below summarises the opinion of budget managers about the relationship between the organisational characteristics and their attitude towards budget system.

TABLE 7.3 **Organisational Characteristics and its Relationship with Budget Manager's Attitude Towards Budget System**

Organisational Characteristics	Attitude Towards Budget System Variables			
	Accounting Control	Game to Play	Cost more than worth	Improve Efficiency
Size	-.108	-.127	.099	-.022
Market	.154	-.034	-.200***	-.096
Diversification	.251*	.100	-.054	.039
Technology	-.006	.213***	-.226**	.138
Autonomy	-.124	.392*	-.136	.247*

* < .01 ** < .02 *** < .05

Table 7.3 reveals that the variables of organisational characteristics - 'Diversification' and 'Autonomy' - are significantly correlated with the variables of budget manager's attitude towards budget system- 'Budget is an accounting tool', 'Budget is a game to play', and 'efficiency can be improved through budgets' - at .01 level of significance. It means that budget becomes a game to play when organisation is decentralized and operational autonomy is granted to operating units.

7.3 ORGANISATIONAL CHARACTERISTICS AND BUDGETEES' JOB SATISFACTION

The opinion of budget managers about the impact of organisational characteristics upon the budgetees' job performance is shown below in Table 7.4.

TABLE 7.4 **Opinion of Budget Managers about the Organisational Characteristics and their Impact upon Budgetees Job Performance**

Organisational Characteristics	Performance Variables			
	Influence Productivity	Stimulate Performance	Work better	Instructions, not budgets
Size	-.162	.059	.112	-.022
Market	.076	-.076	-.082	-.177
Diversification	.089	-.191	-.030	-.179
Technology	-.002	.259*	-.052	-.027
Autonomy	.052	.150	.337*	-.023

* < .01

Table 7.4 indicates that the variables of budgetees job performance - 'budgets stimulate budgetees for better performance', and 'it is possible to work better at reduced costs' - are significantly correlated with the variables of organisational characteristics - 'technology'; and 'autonomy' - at .01 level of significance. It means that the use of better technology in organisation not only stimulates budgetees for better performance but also makes it possible to work better at reduced costs through budgets if operational autonomy is granted to the budgetees in the organisations.

The opinion of budgetees about the impact of organisational characteristics upon budgetee's job performance is summarised below in Table 7.5.

TABLE 7.5 **Relationship Between Organisational Characteristics and Budgetees Job Performance**

Organisational Characteristics	Performance Variables			
	Influence Productivity	Stimulate Performance	Work better	Instructions, not budgets
Size	.105	-.123	.054	-.034
Market	-.001	-.113	-.118	.123
Diversification	-.061	-.008	-.109	.004
Technology	-.056	.127	-.032	.111
Autonomy	-.077	.023	.040	.024

Table 7.5 reveals that none of the variables of organisational characteristics is significantly correlated with the variables of budgetees' job performance even at .05 level of significance.

7.4 ORGANISATIONAL CHARACTERISTICS AND BUDGETEE'S JOB SATISFACTION

The opinion of budget managers about the impact of organisational characteristics upon budgetees' job satisfaction is shown below in Table 7.6.

TABLE 7.6 **Relationship Between Organisational Characteristics and Budgetees Job Satisfaction**

Organisational Characteristics	Job Satisfaction Variables			
	Like	Tension	Enjoy	Pressure
Size	-.052	.065	-.048	-.126
Market	.071	-.161	.086	.072
Diversification	.008	.137	-.031	.069
Technology	.412*	.092	.326*	-.127
Autonomy	.133	.039	.209***	-.139

* < .01; *** < .05

Table 7.6 indicates that the variables of budgetee's job satisfaction - 'budgetees like the department where they work' and 'budgetees enjoy their jobs'- are significantly correlated with the variables of organisational characteristics - 'technology' - at .01 level of significance. This means that the use of better technology is a crucial factor in improving the job satisfaction of the budgetees in the organisations.

The opinion of budgetees about the impact of organisational characteristics upon their job satisfaction is shown below in Table 7.7.

TABLE 7.7 **Organisational Characteristics and Budgetee's Job Satisfaction**

Organisational Characteristics	Job Satisfaction Variables			
	Like	Tension	Enjoy	Pressure
Size	.105	-.115	-.039	.138
Market	.112	-.092	.136	-.037
Diversification	-.081	.066	-.164	.056
Technology	.217*	-.146	.124	-.077
Autonomy	.273*	.097	.058	.085

*** < .01**

Analysis of data given in Table 7.7 reveals that the variables of budgetee's job satisfaction - 'Budgetees like the department where they work' - is significantly correlated with the variables of organisational characteristics - 'technology'; 'autonomy' at .01 level of significance. This indicates that use of technology and autonomy in the organisation boosts the liking of budgetees to work in their departments.

Analysis of results shown in Tables 7.4, 7.5, 7.6 and 7.7 leads to conclude that in the opinion of budget managers, the use of latest technology is the crucial factor in improving the job performance and job satisfaction of budgetees, whereas in the opinion of budgetees none of the variables - size , market, diversification except technology and autonomy is important to improve their job performance and job satisfaction in the organisations.

8

SUMMARY AND CONCLUSIONS

To overcome the lack of conceptual clarity with respect to the usage of the term budgeting, irrelevance of budget standards to the budgetee's task and negative attitude of budgetees towards present budgetary practices followed by companies, an empirical study has been made in this work to design an alternative approach to budget system i.e. playing budgeting as a game that will have potential for high motivation and involvement of budgetees for definite achievements. To delineate it further, the objective of the present study has been three folds:

(a) To record the opinion of budget managers and budgetees about the input factors which directly or indirectly affect the output of budget system;
(b) To diagnose the main problems relating to the perceived characteristics of input factors of budget system; and
(c) To measure the contribution of the inputs of budget system to the final goals of an enterprise. The final goals, i.e., output of the budget system measured in this study are the motivations to all the budgetees for better performance (as a contribution to profitability). and the well-being of budgetees of all ranks (as a contribution to job satisfaction).

The main findings of this study are summarised below.

Job performance and job satisfaction of budgetees as output factors of budget system are found to be most relevant and appropriate variables to judge the profitability to the shareholders and well-being of budgetees of all ranks.

Six dimensions - 'setting of budget standards', 'participation in budget setting', 'superior subordinate relationships', 'line and staff co-operation on budget matters', 'evaluation of budget performance', and 'feedback of performance results' - are identified as significant input factors of budget system with the help of statistical technique known as Factor Analysis.

The study also reveals the specific characteristics of each input factor of budget system that make budget standards relevant to the budgetee's task from low to high and attitude of budgetees from negative to positive. These are : 'goal-congruence','budgetees' control over the means of attaining their budget standards', 'budget conveys knowledge of exact costs for which budgetees are made responsible for', 'tight but attainable standards', 'genuine participation of budgetees in their budget setting', 'finalisation of budget standards upto budgetees' satisfaction', 'independence of career opportunities from budget performance', 'freedom from criticism', 'educative role of staff on budget matters', 'less superior-subordinate conflict', 'self-evaluation of budget performance', 'emphasis upon budgetees' ability to attain budget standards rather than personality traits in performance evaluation', 'understandable performance reports', 'reporting on controllable, responsible and measurable aspects of budgetees' performance', 'budgetees participation in feedback sessions' and 'reporting of performance results to budgetees without delay'.

The contribution of each input variable to job performance and job satisfaction of budgetees is also measured in this study. The study clearly shows that both motivation and job satisfaction of budgetees are positively affected when the atmosphere created around the fulfilment of budget standards is one of the sportsmanship, i.e., playing budgeting as a game. This game atmosphere is related to the control-autonomy balance, because the game presupposes a certain free area to play. Without this freedom there can be no game-spirit. Budgetees need free scope in budget fulfilment.

Personality and cultural background of budgetees also play important role in the job performance and job satisfaction of budgetees. However, low occupational level and longer association with budget system are found to be a source of dissatisfaction among budgetees.

The use of latest technology and operational/technical autonomy find favour in improving the job performance of budgetees in the opinion of both budget managers and budgetees.

The success of budget system largely depends upon its ability to create satisfying and productive teamwork. The significant factors identified as play element in the budget system are : 'more freedom in thc choice of activity', 'freedom from criticism', 'less organisational structure', 'choice of companions', 'fewer status factors', 'less superior-subordinate conflict', and 'more opportunity to be of oneself'.

The successful budget manager is one who can successfully apply these principles while designing a budget system for the organisation and can save the humanity within the system.

SUGGESTIONS FOR IMPLEMENTING BUDGET PROBLEMS

The conclusions of the present study described in the preceding paragraphs, are translated into practical advice for those who have to work and live with budgets and budgetary standards in the organisations. This advice is based upon the situation of a manufacturing company. There are separate implications for:

CHIEF EXECUTIVE

Chief executive must assume an active role in the implementation of budget programs. The most effective manner to implement budgeting is to allow the Top Line executives to explain, co-ordinate and guide the program. When top executives are actively involved, the philosophy and mechanics of the program will filter through and penetrate the entire organisation. Thus, a possible motivation strategy to improve need satisfaction at lower levels of the organisation would be to involve the top level executive group in the budget program.

Another critical factor in the implementation of budget programs is the supportive managerial climate which pervades the organisation. Keeping this objective in view, top level executives who are about to engage in budget programs must first be conditioned and psychologically prepared. With the introduction of budgeting, changes will often occur in organisational variables such as the flow of communication horizontally and vertically, the intensity of intergroup interaction, and the number of personal contacts between superiors and subordinates. Thus, the dynamic nature of these variables and their impact on the functioning of the organisation necessitate complete understanding of budgeting by top level executives to ensure that managerial resistance to implementation and participation is minimal.

BUDGET MANAGERS/INDUSTRIAL ENGINEERS

Budget reports that convey the evaluation of budgetees' performance must be sufficiently understandable to the budgetees, otherwise it will create more problems than solving them. Sufficiently understandable reports help budgetees in improving their performance.

Evaluation of budgetees performance must be based upon their ability to attain budget standards rather than personality traits of the budgetees. This will not only make the job enjoyable but also reduce pressure on budgetees.

Budgetees' career opportunities should be kept independent of their budgeted performance as far as possible. Independence of career opportunities from budgeted performance will invoke budgetees to improve their performance and keep them free from pressure on the job.

Budgets should be such that can help budgetees in knowing exact costs for which they are made responsible through budgets. Knowledge of exact costs through budgets stimulates budgetees for better performance and improve their liking to work in the department where they are working.

Budgetees must be allowed to exercise greater degree of influence in the determination of their budget standards. Exercising of greater influence in the determination of own budgets not only influences the productivity of budgetees but also makes it possible for them to work better at reduced costs.

Budgets improve budgetees' linking to work in the department in which they are working provided the technology of the department is to be rated as one of the best or above average.

Budgets should be prepared in such a way that convinces budgetees about the importance of meeting not only the quantity standards but also the quality of budget standards. This will certainly stimulate budgetees for better performance.

Budgets should be such that extract greater efforts on the part of budgetees through the use of skill and technical know-how in meeting the production schedules.

Feedback must follow closely to the actions of budgetees. This has greater significance in influencing and stimulating budgetees for working better at reduced costs.

Involve budgetees in the setting of their budget standards so that they feel a real sense of satisfaction in the attainment of budget standards. This will not only induce and stimulate budgetees for better performance but also improve budgetees' liking and enjoyment of the department as well as the job respectively.

Budgetees participation in feedback sessions influences and stimulates budgetees for better performance at reduced costs. Hence budgetees should be allowed to participate where their budget performance is evaluated.

As far as possible budget should be clear and accurate to the budgetees because it has a direct bearing on the liking of budgetees to the department where they work.

While setting the budget standards for budgetees, provision should be made for greater use of efforts, skill and technical know-how on their part to attain budget standards. Though this make them under tension initially but ultimately improve the liking of the budgetees where they work and also make their job enjoyable.

As far as possible, budgets must be finalised to the satisfaction of budgetees. Otherwise budgetees feel alienated on their jobs.

While allowing budgetees to participate in the setting of their budget standards, care should be taken in diagnosing the attitude of budgetees towards participation. Favourable attitude of budgetees towards participation in budget setting stimulates budgetees for better performance and avoids stress and tension on the job.

Reporting of performance evaluation is a must at least for those areas for which budgetees are responsible. Knowledge of results to the budgetees improves their performance and stimulates budgetees for better performance. Moreover, knowledge of results makes the job enjoyable to budgetees and avoids tension and nervousness on the job.

Budget should be such that makes budgetees less dependent on superiors in their operations. This will make budgetees less agitated and nervous on the job.

Train people who are associated with budget department about behavioural aspects of budget system so that this department can work as an autonomous planning commission to formulate and monitor budget system that can stimulate budgetees for better performance.

Feedback of performance evaluation should be restricted to areas where performance can be measured adequately. This avoids subjectivity in the measurement of budgetees' performance and induces budgetees for better performance and thus reduces pressure on their jobs.

Budget managers must educate budgetees on budget matters as much as possible without delay and hesitation. Smooth co-operation between line and staff on budget matters not only improves the liking of budgetees to work in the department where they are working but also makes their jobs enjoyable.

LINE MANAGERS/MARKETING/OPERATING

Line managers should appreciate rather reject any idea or suggestion suggested by line subordinates about budget matters or the areas of their work which is directly or indirectly concerned with the working of budget system. Rejection of budgetees' ideas not only puts them under pressure on the job but also has negative effect on their job performance.

Line managers should take care of private interests of line subordinates while setting budget standards for them. This leads to influence their budgeted performance and avoids nervousness and tension on the job.

Listening of subordinates' suggestions by their top line management with an attitude of fair consideration induces budgetees to work better at reduced costs.

Line managers should persuade budgetees rather than to dictate them on budget matters. This will instill confidence in line subordinates and will result in performing better at reduced costs.

Line managers should encourage budgetees' co-operation over budget matters without hesitation. This will invoke confidence in them and that will result ultimately in influencing and stimulating them for better performance and reduce their tension and nervousness on the job.

Top line managers should allow budgetees to exercise greater control over the means of attaining their budget standards. This will improve budgetees' enjoyment of job while performing better at reduced costs.

PERSONNEL MANAGERS

Budgetees who believe in the culture of obedience and respect for elders and accept superiors' decisions without reservation prefer to work in such department and enjoy their job.

Budgetees who were less willing to carry responsibilities than they used to be always feel under pressure and tention on the job.

More pressure on the job is experienced by those budgetees who are associated with the budget system for longer period.

Younger rather elder budgetees feel more stimulated through budgets for better performance.

The variable - 'obedience and respect are important virtues children should learn' - is found favour in the opinion of budgetees. It means the culture of respect for elders while working in the organisation, not only stimulates budgetees for better performance but also influences their liking to the department where they are working.

Higher status of budgetees is associated with pressure on the job. This is obvious due to the increased responsibilities. However, it did not show any sign of dissatisfaction.

LIMITATIONS AND EXTENSIONS OF THE RESEARCH

The study has both some obvious limitations as well as some natural extensions discussed as under:

First, a theoretical model has been developed in chapter 3 to identify some of the important variables and to hypothesize some general relationships between them. There was little in the way of empirical and theoretical work that could help us in developing this model. This placed severe limitations on our ability to formulate specific hypotheses about the relationships between these variables and led us to make general rather specific assertions about these relationships. Due to paucity of previous work, it would have been pretentious for us to do otherwise. Taken as otherwise, our empirical findings tend to confirm the general pattern of relationships implied by the theoretical model. A natural extension of the study is the further confirmation of the variables contained in our model and posting of specific hypotheses about the relationships between them. The crucial aspect of the model which remains to be validated in future research is the direction of the relationships depicted in the model.

Second, the results of this study are based on a situation of a manufacturing company. Hence this study can be extended to other than manufacturing units of the business. It can also be extended from top level management to the non-management employees level and the non-business organisations.

Third, approach of the study has been essentially a 'transversal', i.e., each organisation is studied only at one moment in time. It would be very attractive to carry out a 'longitudinal' study of budgeting effects; to follow a particular organisation through various stages of the budget cycle. However, within the available time,this did not prove feasible. An appropriate extension of our research would be an investigation of the relationships depicted in our model through various stages of budget cycle.

Fourth, the research design adopted for the study is also subject to some limitations. The field study research design has the distinct advantage of allowing data to be obtained from managers operating in the real existing organisations of the kind of which the results are intended to apply. However, this advantage is gained at the cost of less precision, less control and less freedom to manipulate variables whose effects may be of central concern. Although field experiments are difficult to perform successfully, their value as a research strategy should not be underestimated. Only through the field experiments, the findings of rigorous, well controlled laboratory experiments can be tested for their applicability to natural organisational settings. An appropriate extension of our research would be an investigation of the relationships depicted in our model in more controlled and experimentally manipulated settings.

Finally, in implementing the overall research design, the data were collected through personal interviews, company records and the questionnaires. However, the questionnaires were based on Likert-Scale to obtain data from budget managers and budgetees about their budget-oriented behaviour and its impact upon budgetees' job satisfaction and job performance. Likert-Scale has been criticised since the same score for two individuals does not necessarily indicate that they carry the same attitude. Nonetheless, the scale enjoys wide usage with convincing results and hence has been used appropriately (and with caution) in this study. Natural extension of our research may indicate the use of alternative ways of obtaining the data about some of the variables included in the study, the development of improved measures of these variables and the use of alternative means of analysis.

Appendix I

QUESTIONNAIRE FOR BUDGET MANAGERS

A-RESPONDENT'S PROFILE

1. a Official title of your present job ....
   b Number of years with this company ....
   c Number of years in the present job ....
   d Age at interview date (in years) ....
   e Educational qualifications ....
   f Have you ever attended management development programme
     * Yes
     * No
   g Did it deal with budgeting or standard setting
     * Yes
     * No
   h What is your present job consists of ....
   i Which part of your job do you consider most important; and ....
   j Why ....

B-CORPORATE CHARACTERISTICS

2. a Are your company's operations primarily (Please tick)
     * Manufacturing
     * Non-manufacturing
     * Service
     * Non-service
     * Others, specify
   b List the name of five principal products/services (please name)
     1.
     2.
     3.
     4.
     5.
   c Number of employees ....
   d Annual sales or equivalent (in crores of Rupees) ....

e Indicate the marketing areas dominated by your Organisation
* International
* National
* State
* Local
* None

f Indicate the complexities of your business activities (Please tick)
* Single business (not diversified
* Dominated business
* Related business
* Non-related business (diversified
* Others, specify

g How would you classify the firm in which you are working as one that could be an example for the application of advanced technological methods (Please tick)
* As one of the best
* Above average
* Average
* Lower than average
* Not good
* One of the worst

h Name of the company divisions, sub-divisions, or subsidiaries, each of which performance is definitely measured in terms of profit contribution (Please name)

Divisions	Sub-divisions	Subsidiaries	
....	....	....	....
....	....	....	....
....	....	....	....
....	....	....	....
....	....	....	....
....	....	....	....

i What is the degree of decentralisation of managerial authority in your company (Please tick the most appropriate)
* Divisional, subsidiary or plant managers have full authority and responsibility for their operations in a manner similar to a separate company except for broad overall policy, control and appraisal of results

* Divisional, Subsidiary or plant managers have considerable authority and responsibility for their operation and are expected to develop operational plans and control procedures in detail, subject to continuous review and approval by central management.

* Divisional, Subsidiary and plant managers carry out operational plans or budgets developed in detail by central management
* Others, specify

j How would you rank the significance attached to the given objectives in your organisation (Please rank)
Rank objectives:
* Profitability
* Market position
* Productivity

			* Product leadership * Personnel development * Employee attitudes * Social responsibility * Others, specify

C-PLANNING

3.	a	Does your company establish a short range profit objective for the company as a whole for a definite period of one year or less	* Yes * No
			* Written * Informal
	b	If yes, please indicate what individuals or groups formally approve the profit objective (Please tick)	* Board of Directors * Chairman/President of the Board * Controller/Vice-President Finance * Executive/Management Committee * Director Finance/Executive * Others, specify
	c	Specify length of period	....
4.		In what other principal areas definite (budget) objectives or goals are established? Please indicate by ticking the areas of the budget and the title of the individual or groups primarily responsible for developing (as opposed to final approval) the same	Area of Budgets Title of the people responsible for developing * Sales............................ .. .. * Expenses........................ .... * Production....................... .... * Capital Exp...................... .... * Raw material..................... .... * Research.......................... ...... * Advertising .... * Cash .... * Others, specify ....
5.		In general, how are the definite (budgets) objectives or goals indicated in question No. 3 (a) and 4 established? (Please tick one)	* Goals and objectives are developed by higher levels of management & are presented to subordinate level of management for their consideration and comment prior to final adoption * Goals and objectives are established exclusively by members of higher management without consultation with subordinate level of management. * Subordinate level of management are requested to submit goals and objectives relating to their par-

			ticular functions for review and final approval by their higher levels of management. * Others, Specify
6.	a	Are objectives and goals indicated in question 3(a) and 4 included in detail plan of operations (or budgets)	* Yes * No
	b	If yes, how often is the plan of operations (or budgets) reviewed for possible revision (Please tick)	* Monthly * Quarterly * Half-yearly * Annually * Others, specify
7.	a	Indicate the general areas in which your company makes formal long range forecasts or plans, that is for periods of more than one year. Indicate also the length in years of each forecast or plan.	Areas of Forecasts — Periods * Sales ....years * Capital Expenditure ....years * Profits ....years * Research ....years * Expenses ....years * Cash ....years * Others, specify ....years
	b	How often are your company's long range forecasts or plans modi-fied or revised (Please tick)	* Annually * As needed * Others, specify
	a	How does your company convey to each executive or supervisor a clear understanding of the responsibilities of his department included in the plan of operations (or budgets)? (please tick)	* Formal conferences * Informal conferences * Copy of operational plans * Others, specify
	b	If formal conferences are used, who usually conducts such conferences (Please tick)	* Primarily staff with some line assistance * Primarily line with some staff assistance * Line and staff participating on equal basis * Staff personnel only * Line personnel only * Others, specify
	a	Do you have a budget committee or its equivalent	* Yes * No
	b	If no, what group or individual co-ordinates the principal budget activities	....
		Indicate the title of the individual primarily responsible for financial expression of the com-	* Chairman/President * Budget Director * Controller

	bined objectives and goals of the various organisational units in a co-ordinated plan of operations or budgets for top management (Please tick)	* Advisor-Finance * Director-Finance * Others, specify	
11.	Indicate the type and period of forecasts which are developed in your organisation (Please tick)	Types of Forecasts	Periods
		* General economic conditions	....
		* Sales estimate of the company	....
		* Sales estimates of the industry	....
		* Share of market	....
		* Others, specify	....
12.	What are the principal procedures or techniques used in making your sales forecasts (Please tick)	* Past sales trend of the company * Salesman's estimate * New product line * Market surveys * Production capacity * Industry forecasts and your share * Promotion Plans * Financial capacity * Outside consultation * Competitor's activity * Sales with economic trends * Others, specify	

D-CONTROL

13.	To whom you are reporting	....	
14.	Who are the people immediately reporting to you and what jobs do they have	People	Their jobs
		....	....
		....	....
		....	....
		....	....
15.	Indicate the techniques used in your company for overall control of company performance (Please tick)	* Budgetary Control * Return on capital employed * Direct observation * Break-even analysis * Cash forecasts * Profit control * Conferences * Others, specify	
16.	Check the items which are used as a standard (or yardstick) in your company to measure, to control and/or to evaluate current sales or service revenues	* Historical data * Sales forecasts * Sales budget * Sales quotas * Others, specify	

(Please tick)

17.	a	Indicate the items which are used as a standard (or yardstick) in your company to measure, to control and/or to evaluate current costs and expenses (Please tick all used)	* Historical costs * Labour standards * Material standards * Standard costs * Cost ratios * Direct costs * Others, specify
	b	If expense standards or expense budgets are used to evaluate actual current performance, which group or groups are principally responsible for initiating and approving them (Please tick all appropriates)	Costs Initiates Approves * Material costs .... * Labour costs .... * Factory overheads .... * Admini.overheads .... * Selling overheads .... * Distribution overheads . ... * Others, specify ....
	c	If expense standards or budgets are not initiated or approved by executives or supervisors responsibile for functions involved, to what extent are such executives or supervisors consulted concerning the expense standards finally approved (Please tick)	* Not at all * Ask for review and comment; opinion given little weight * Asked for review and comment; opinions given considerable weight * Asked for review and comment, opinions almost always accepted * Others, specify
18.		Are detailed expense budget (or plans) prepared for (Please tick)	* Direct material costs * Direct labour costs * Factory overheads * Administrative overheads * Selling overheads * Distribution overheads * Others, specify
19.		To what extent do your control reports covering current results follow organisational authority and responsibility (Please tick)	* Fully * Substantially * Partially * Not at all
20.	a	Is a separate report comparing actual performance with standards of performance or budget objective prepared for each department or its equivalent	* Yes * No
	b	If yes, please tick the types of reports prepared and also indicate the frequency of their preparation	Types of reports Frequency * Sales .... * Profit .... * Cash .... * Factory overheads .... * Administrative overheads .... * Selling overheads .... * Distribution overheads ....

			* Others, specify ....
21.		Where a report shows a significant deviation from the company's standards of performance or budget, does your company require (Please tick whichever is applicable)	* Written explanation of the causes of such deviations * An indication of corrective action taken * A discussion or deviation with immediate supervisor * An oral explanation * Others, specify
22.	a	Please indicate the broad cate guries of expenses listed in which your company identifies the fixed and variable components of each individual expenses	* Factory overheads * Administrative overheads * Selling overheads * Distribution overheads * Others, specify
	b	If yes, please check the method or methods used to identify these components (Please tick)	* Graphic analysis * Direct analysis * Direct observation * Engineering analysis * Methods of least squares * Others, specify
23.		Please indicate the broad categories of expenses listed in which your company identifies as con trollable or uncontrollable (Please tick)	* Factory overheads * Administrative overheads * Selling overheads * Distribution overheads * Others, specify
24.	a	In your company do you have regular meetings of management groups primarily to discuss and compare actual performance with planned performance	* Yes * No
	b	If yes, please indicate at what management levels this is done (Please tick)	* Board of Directors * Top management executives * Executive committee * Deptt. or Division committee * Plant management * Supervisor * Others, specify

25.	Who has the responsibility for following up and for taking corrective action on unfavourable deviations from standards or budgets (Please tick)	Authorities	Follow up	Corrective action
		* Budget Director	....	....
		* Budget committee	......	....
		* Controller	....	....
		* Supervisor	....	....
		* Others, specify	....	....

26.		Which of the views indicated are expressive of your top management's view on budget standards of performance as control device (Please tick)	* They represent procedure which can be used effectively to exert pressure to improve efficiency and output * They represent procedure which should be used to motivate subordinates to increase efficiency and output through participation * They represent procedure which does motivate subordinates but primarily increases efficiency through pressure * They represent procedure which does exert some pressure on subordinates but primarily increases efficiency through motivation * Others, specify

E-MISCELLANEOUS

27.		Do you have a formal budget programme in your company	* Yes * No
		If yes, please answer the following questions:	
	a	Title of the person supervising or directing the budget system	....
	b	Title of person to whom he reports	
	c	Do you have a budget manual or its equivalent	* Yes * No
	d	What period of time does your budget or plan of operations cover and how it is broken down by interim time periods (Please tick)	* Annually, broken down by months * Annually, broken down by quarters * Quarterly, broken down by months * Six-monthly, broken down by months * Others, specify
	e	How is the budget profit and loss statement sub-divided (please tick)	* Do not prepare * By-product lines * Monthly * Annually * For major sub-divisions only * Others, specify
	f	If break-even analysis is prepared, tick the area for which it is prepared	* For company as a whole * For various divisions * For plant * For product line

		* For sales branches * Others, specify
g	To what extent budget system evolved by your company is con tributing to the achievement of your organisational goals	* To a maximum degree * To a great degree * To a moderate degree * To a minor degree * Not at all
28.	What were the principal problems encountered by your firm in developing budgets and budgetary controls	....
29.	Please make any other comments about the system that you feel are not adequately treated/ covered in the above questionnaire	....

F-ATTITUDE SURVEY-STAFF OFFICERS

With the experience of budgeting and business judgement regarding other control techniques that you might have come across, you might have formed certain opinions/impressions about the effectiveness of budgetary control system in maximising the possible contribution to the achievements of organisational goals. Please read each of the following sentences relating to various aspects of budgeting and rate on every scale by ticking such that you feel most appropriate. All replies are left to your business judgement and experience. For each sentence, the answer scale is the same.

Always	Mostly	Sometimes	Seldom	Never
1	2	3	4	5
*	*	*	*	*

NOTE: It is explained to participants that in each case where this scale does not apply literally, e. g., 'mostly' must be read as 'agreement in most cases'.

	SENTENCES	Always	Mostly	Some times	Seldom	Never
1	I like the department I work in	*	*	*	*	*
2	Budgeting is first of all an accounting tool	*	*	*	*	*
3	Working comes naturally to most people	*	*	*		*
4	The line managers are ignorant about the job done by my department	*	*	*	*	*
5	In this organisation, my private inter ests are taken account of as much as possible	*	*	*	*	*
6	Staff department should leave more to the line	*	*	*	*	*
7	My job makes me agitated and nervous	*	*	*	*	*

8 The line managers are insufficiently cost conscious
9 The directives from Head Office are limited to necessary minimum
10 The first task of my department is service to management
11 I enjoy my job
12 The co-operation between line and staff department is smooth
13 Performance of managers is justly appraised here on their ability to attain budgets
14 Obedience and respect for authority are the important virtues children should learn
15 People now-a-days are less willing to carry responsibility then they used to be
16 This organisation is well managed
17 My seniors ask my opinions about matters concerning my areas of work
18 A main task of budget variance report is to show seniors where their subordinates have failed
19 In my department too, efficiency can be improved
20 Line management is sufficiently conscious of the need for reliable clerical data
21 A clear order is better than consultation
22 Line management is well convinced of the importance of meeting quality standards
23 This department demands my guidance
24 Young people sometimes get rebellious ideas, but as they grow up they ought to get over them and settle down
25 It is possible to work much better and at less cost in this department
26 More co-operation is desired between my department and the line managers
27 I feel pressure in my job
28 My career opportunities here depend first of all on myself
29 My department is insufficiently consulted in organisational problems
30 Subordinates ought to accept their senior's decisions without reservation
31 The line managers do not spend enough efforts to meet production schedules
32 Line management follows our advice
33 Budgeting motivates the line to work towards the company goals
34 Budgeting is one of the best tools yet

devised for advancing the affairs of the company

35 Reporting of budget information follows closely upon the action

36 Most managers feel a real sense of accomplishment when they meet their budgets

37 Reporting of budget information is limited to behaviour controllable by the receivers

38 Budgets are yardsticks used to evaluate performance

39 Seniors encourage the line to use staff effectively

40 Seniors recognise that time and efforts spent in training and educating managers by staff is an excellent investment

41 Seniors appreciate the suggestions regarding process techniques in this organisation

42 Managers quickly learn to play the budget game

43 Seniors hesitate in taking my co-operation on budget matters

44 Budgeting tends to make employees feel dependent on seniors

45 Budgeting gives too much power to Financial Department

46 Budgeting forces managers to bargain with the Financial Department

47 Budgeting tends to take away the freedom of the line supervisors

48 Reporting of budget information is within the receivers' responsibility

49 Budget system costs a lot more than they are worth

50 Budget stimulates managers for better performance without enslaving them

51 Feedback is limited to areas where adequate performance is possible

52 Receivers of budget information participate in the feedback process

53 Budgeting helps line in knowing exactly which cost they are responsible for

54 I think our budget goals are clear and accurate

55 I prefer the budget that can easily be achieved.

56 Our budget requires a great deal of efforts from line to attain them

57 Budgeting requires high degree of

	skill and know-how on line manager's part to attain them	•	•	•	•	•
58	Line managers have absolute control over the means of reaching their department's budget	•	•	•	•	•
59	Budget is not finalised until I am satisfied with that	•	•	•	•	•
60	I allow high degree of influence in the determination of budget standards to those who have to attain budgets	•	•	•	•	•
61	Budgets have favourable attitudes towards participation	•	•	•	•	•
62	Line managers are personally held accountable for budget variances in their department	•	•	•	•	•
63	We express our dissatisfaction when line managers show negative variances	•	•	•	•	•
64	Analysis of budget variances were concerned only with physical targets	•	•	•	•	•
65	Line managers attend meetings where budget variances are discussed	•	•	•	•	•
66	Budget variances are considered as factors in raising of manager's pay	•	•	•	•	•
67	I am clear about the limits of my authority in present position	•	•	•	•	•
68	I am clear about the expectations of the people around me	•	•	•	•	•
69	I enjoyed participating in this research project	•	•	•	•	•

Appendix II

QUESTIONNAIRE FOR BUDGETEES

A-RESPONDENT'S PROFILE

1.	a	Official title of your present job	....
	b	Number of years with this company	....
	c	Number of years in the present job	....
	d	Age at interview date (in years)	....
	e	Educational qualifications	....
	f	Have you ever attended management development programme	* Yes * No
	g	Did it deal with budgeting or standard setting	* Yes * No
	h	What is your present job consists of	....
	i	Which part of your job do you consider most important; and	....
	j	Why	....

B-CORPORATE CHARACTERISTICS

2.	a	Is your company's operations primarily (Please tick)	* Manufacturing * Non-manufacturing * Service * Non-service * Others, specify
	b	List the name of five principal products/services (Please name)	1. 2. 3. 4. 5.
	c	Number of employees	....
	d	Annual sales or equivalent (in crores of Rupees)	....
	e	Indicate the marketing areas dominated by your Organisation	* International * National * State * Local * None
	f	Indicate the complexities of	* Single business (not diversified)

	your business activities (Please tick)	* Dominated business * Related business * Non-related business (diversified) * Others, specify	
g	How would you classify the firm in which you are working as one that could be an example for the application of advanced technological methods (Please tick)	* As one of the best * Above average * Average * Lower than average * Not good * One of the worst	

		Divisions	Sub-divisions	Subsidiaries
h	Name of the company divisions, sub-divisions, or subsidiaries each of which performance is definitely measured in terms of profit contribution (Please name)	....	....	....
		....	....	....
		....	....	....
		....	....	....
		....	....	....

i	What is the degree of decentralisation of managerial authority in your company (Please tick the most appropriate)	* Divisional, subsidiary or plant managers have full authority and responsibility for their operations in a manner similar to a separate company except for broad overall policy, control and appraisal of results * Divisional, subsidiary or plant managers have considerable authority and responsibility for their operation and are expected to develop operational plans and control procedures in detail, subject to continuous review and approval by central management * Divisional, subsidiary and plant managers carry out operational plans or budgets developed in detail by central management * Others, specify
j	How would you rank the significance attached to the given objectives in your organisation (Please rank)	Rank objectives: * Profitability * Market position * Productivity * Product leadership * Personnel development * Employee attitudes * Social responsibility * Others, specify

C-PLANNING

3.	a	Does your company establish standards for your job	* Yes * No * Written

		* Informal
b	To what extent are the standards for your job what you personally think they ought to be? (Please tick)	* Exactly the same * Very much the same * Mostly the same but some are different * Half the same/half different * Mostly different * Have no clearly defined goals
c	To what extent did the performance goals set for you under the budget programme, reflect the most serious and pressing needs of your department (Please tick)	* To a maximum extent * To a great extent * To a moderate extent * To a minor extent * Not at all
d	In my opinion, budgets/goals of my department represent the following view point (Please tick)	* Clear, concise and unambiguous * Accurate in terms of the true end-state * Consistent with the company policies * Interesting, motivating and challenging * Within the competence of the man * Others, specify
e	At what levels of your budgets (standards) are set (Please tick)	* Chairman/President of the Board * Executive/Financial Vice-President * Executive/Management Committee * Board of Directors * Controller * Others, specify
f	Do you think your standards are tight or loose here (Please tick)	* Too loose * Fairly loose * Just right * Tight but attainable * Too tight
4.	What kinds of special plans do you have for your department in the coming year	....
5.	Five cards are given, Please rank them in the sequence in which they demand your attention (Please rank)	* Leading the personnel * Fulfilling the production schedules * Maintaining the quality * Keeping cost down * Developing new product and processes * Others, specify

			Minor	Moderate	Maximum	Rank
6.	Eight cards are given. Please divide them into three groups	Areas of influence				
		Direct material				

and rank the cards in the third group as to the degree of influence your department has on them

costs	*	*	*	*
Direct labour costs	*	*	*	*
Reject costs	*	*	*	*
Factory overheads	*	*	*	*
Administrative overheads	*	*	*	*
Selling overheads	*	*	*	*
Distribution over-heads	*	*	*	*
Others, specify	*	*	*	*

7. Can you influence yourself budgeted efficiency in your department

* Yes
* No

Which areas in particular ....

8. What kind of factors outside your reach also influence budgeted efficiency in your department

....
....
....
....

9. Please estimate the influence of various people on budgeted efficiency in your department on the given scale

People/Degree of Influence	Maxi mum	Mode-rate	Minor	Not at all
Seniors	*	*	*	*
Myself	*	*	*	*
Staff	*	*	*	*
Juniors	*	*	*	*
Others, specify	*	*	*	*

10. Is the above rating of influence equally applicable to technical standards of your department

* Yes
* No

If nc, then whose influence is more important in setting technical standards

....
....
....

11. How are budget standards set in your department. Please estimate your role and also desirable role in the budget setting

	As it is		As desirable	
Type of Role	Myself	Staff	Myself	Staff
Decision taken by me/them without consultation	*	*	*	*
Proposed by me/them followed by consultation; /their opinions generally prevail	*	*	*	*
Proposed by me/them, decision made jointly	*	*	*	*
Proposed by				

		others, my/their opinion asked & has a lot of Weight * * *
		My/their opinion not asked but decision explained to me/them * * **
		My/their opinion not asked; decision explained to me/them.
12.	Do you think that the performance of your department will improve in the coming year	* Yes * No
	Which areas in particular Please give reasons	....

D-CONTROL

13.	To whom you are reporting	....
14.	Who are the people immediately reporting to you. What jobs do they have	People / Their jobs ....
15.	How frequently do you get information about the performance of your department	Daily/Weekly/Monthly/Quarterly/ Six-monthly/Annually/Not at all available
	What is the source	....
16.	What is your impression about the management information System followed in your department (Please tick whichever is appropriate)	* The reports are received too late * Budget allowances are not adjusted to the actual level of out-put * Reports do not include the real reasons of poor performance * Expenses which are not controllable are included without indication * Reports always seem to emphasize errors, weaknesses and failures * The time spans covered by the performance reports are too much * The performance reports are used primarily as a pressure device * Standards are unrealistically high and therefore comparison is not useful * Reports do not reflect achievement, trust, loyalty, dedication of the

			human resources * None of the above * Others, specify
17.	a	Do you have regular meetings with your seniors and colleagues	* Yes * No
	b	If yes, how often	Daily/Weekly/Forthnightly/ Monthly/As needed/Others
	c	Who participates	....
	d	What topics are discussed	....
	e	Which statement best describes the utility of these meetings (Please tick whichever is appropriate)	* Conveying own feelings to seniors * Correctly perceiving effects of own behaviour on others * Correctly understanding effects of others behaviour on self * Hearing others and accepting helpful criticism * Appropriately interacting with others * Formality * Others, specify
18.		Do you have similar meetings with your subordinates. Which statement best describes the utility of these meetings (Please tick whichever is appropriate)	* Establishing meaningful interpersonal relationship * Finding a satisfying place among subordinates * Understanding dynamic complexities in subordinates behaviour * Developing diagnostic skills to understand subordinates problems and processes * Acquiring skills of helping subordinates on tasks and maintenance problems * Formality * Others, specify
19.		Do your seniors discuss budget variances or other performance figures of your department with you	* Yes * No
		Which figures in particular	....
20.	a	Do you receive budget variance reports, if any	* Yes * No
	b	What types of reports	....
	c	How frequently	Daily/Weekly/Forthnightly/ Monthly/Others
	d	From whom	....
	e	What figures in them do you study in particular	....
	f	What use do you make of these figures	....

21.		What is your general impression about the budget reports sent to you in the presentation of budget information (Please tick whichever is most appropriate)	* Reports are unduly cumbersome and containing a lot of irrelevant information * Reports are fairly simple in design but as they do not focus on the controllable aspect of my performance, I find it difficult to act on the basis of these reports * The reports are simple and present relevant information but for some reason or the other, I am unable to use them * The reports are clear, specific and deal with the controllable aspects of my performance. I am, therefore, able to take purposeful action on the basis of these reports * Others, specify
22.		What is your general impression about the follow up action taken by your seniors on performance aspects (Please tick)	* There is no follow up action by my seniors. Reports are filed as soon as they are submitted * There is occasional follow-up by my seniors. Now and then he asks me why certain items have gone out of control * There is frequent follow-up by my seniors. I am called upon to explain adverse variances from standards and initiate corrective action * There is very systematic and purposeful follow up action taken by my seniors * Others, specify
23.	a	With whom in the Budget/Finance/Controller's department do you have contacts	....
	b	How often	Daily/Weekly/Forthnightly/Monthly/Others
	c	About what subjects	....
	d	How wholesome relationship do you have with these people	* Very satisfactory * Quite satisfactory * Fairly satisfactory * A little satisfactory * Very dissatisfied
24.		With what other departments do you have contact	....
		How often	Daily/Weekly/Forthnightly/Monthly/Others
		About what subjects	....
		How is your relationship with	Very/Quite/Fairly/A little/Not at

	them	all satisfactory
25.	What are the most important improvements that could presently be made in your department	....

26. Do the standards that are set here influence productivity in this plant/department
* Yes
* No

Which areas in particular ....

27. How do you judge a person's consciousness towards

Cost	Quality	Budget
....	....	....
....	....	....
....	....	....
....	....	....
....	....	....

28. Who appraises your performance ....
In evaluating your performance, how much importance do you think the appraiser attaches to each of the following items
(Please tick one answer on each line)

Areas of Approval	Importance Attached				
	Very	Quite	Some	A Little	Not at all
The efforts I put into my job	*	*	*	*	*
How much profit I make	*	*	*	*	*
My concern with quality	*	*	*	*	*
How well I meet my budget	*	*	*	*	*
The relationship I have with my staff	*	*	*	*	*
How efficiently I run my unit	*	*	*	*	*
My attitude towards my work	*	*	*	*	*
How well I get on with group members	*	*	*	*	*
Others, specify	*	*	*	*	*

29. Please give an evaluation of how your department is performing at present on the following points
(Tick for each line whichever is appropriate)

Performance Areas	Performance Attainded				
	So-so	Satis-	Fairly	Good	Excel-

		factory	good		lent
Material use	*	*	*	*	*
Direct labour	*	*	*	*	*
Reject rate	*	*	*	*	*
Indirect material	*	*	*	*	*
Indirect labour	*	*	*	*	*
Production schedules	*	*	*	*	*
Quality standards	*	*	*	*	*
Others, specify	*	*	*	*	*

30.	Please rate your direct subordinates' performance on the given scale for overall contribution in the performance of your department (Please tick)	* So-so * Satisfactory * Fairly good * Good * Excellent
31.	To what extent budget system evolved by your company as a control device is contributing to the achievement of your organisational goals	* To a maximum degree * To a great degree * To a minor degree * To a moderate degree * Not at all

E-ATTITUDE SURVEY

With the experience of budgeting and business judgement regarding other control techniques that you might have come across, you might have formed certain opinions/impressions about the effectiveness of budgetary control system in maximising the possible contribution to the achievement of organisational goals. Please read each of the following sentences relating to various aspects of budgeting and rate on every scale by ticking such that you feel most appropriate. All replies are left to your business judgement and experience. For each sentence, the answer scale is the same.

Always	Mostly	Sometimes	Seldom	Never
1	2	3	4	5
*	*	*	*	*

(It is explained to participants that in each case where this scale does not apply literally, e.g., 'mostly' must be read as 'agreement in most cases').

SENTENCES	Always	Mostly	Sometimes	Seldom	Never
1. I like the department I work in	......	......	......	......	......
2. Budgeting is first of all an accounting tool	......	......	......	......	......
3. Working comes naturally to most people	......	......	......	......	......
4. My seniors reject my ideas for improvement	......	......	......	......	......
5. In this plant, my private interest are taken account of as much as possible	......	......	......	......	......
6. The management information					

	reports I get are sufficiently understandable	......	......	......	......	......
7.	My job makes me agitated and nervous	......	......	......	......	......
8.	Budgets are set here without taking sufficient account of my department's problems	......	......	......	......	......
9.	I can work as well, without standards/budgets	......	......	......	......	......
10.	If I am absent for a week, my department still keeps running well	......	......	......	......	......
11.	I enjoy my job	......	......	......	......	......
12.	Staff takes no interest in the goal setting programme of my department	......	......	......	......	......
13.	I think my performance is justly appraised here on my ability to attain standards	......	......	......	......	......
14.	Obedience and respect for authority are the most important virtues children should learn	......	......	......	......	......
15.	People now-a-days are less willing to carry responsibilities than they used to be	......	......	......	......	......
16.	This plant is well managed	......	......	......	......	......
17.	My seniors ask my opinions about matters concerning my areas of work	......	......	......	......	......
18.	I think trying to attain standards is a sport	......	......	......	......	......
19.	My seniors are working continuously on cost reduction	......	......	......	......	......
20.	The people from the controller's department have a lack of understanding of my problems	......	......	......	......	......
21.	A clear order is better than consultation	......	......	......	......	......
22.	My seniors listen to my suggestions and complaints with an attitude of fair consideration	......	......	......	......	......
23.	This plant demands my guidance	......	......	......	......	......
24.	Young people sometimes get rebellious ideas, but as they grow up they ought to get over them and settle down	......	......	......	......	......
25.	It would be possible to work much better and at less cost in this plant	......	......	......	......	......
26.	The co-operation between the line and industrial engineers leaves much to be desired	......	......	......	......	......
27.	I feel pressure in my job	......	......	......	......	......
28.	My career opportunities here					

depend first of all on myself ....

29. Taking everything into account, my department runs efficiently enough ....
30. My seniors hold me personally accountable for budget variances in my department ....
31. Subordinates ought to accept their senior's decisions without reservation ....
32. Budgeting helps me in knowing exactly which costs I am responsible for ....
33. Introducing budgeting has improved efficiency in my department ....
34. Seniors take personal interest in the budgetary problems of my department ....
35. I attend meetings of top management where budget variances are discussed ....
36. The budget is primarily developed to meet my department's interests first ....
37. I think my budget goals are ambiguous and not very clear ....
38. I exercise a maximum degree of influence in the determination of my budget goals ....
39. I receive considerable amount of information about my budget achievements ....
40. If I am given a choice, I would prefer to work without standards ....
41. I prefer the standards that may be easily attainable ....
42. My seniors accept my budgets without reservations ....
43. I have really little voice in the formation of my budget goals ....
44. Budget reports appraising performance are shown to me without delay ....
45. Standards stimulated me for better performance ....
46. My budget goals are quite difficult to attain ....
47. I have complete autonomy in making decisions relating to my department's budgets ....
48. I understand fully which of my budget goals are more important

	than others	......	......	......	......	......
49.	My budget is not finalised until I am satisfied with it	......	......	......	......	......
50.	My seniors tell me about how well I am doing in terms of achieving my budget goals	......	......	......	......	......
51.	My budget goals require a great deal of efforts from me to achieve them	......	......	......	......	......
52.	Budgeting requires high degree of skill and know-how on my part to attain them	......	......	......	......	......
53.	If no standards were set, but instructions would be given, this would make my department's performance higher than now	......	......	......	......	......
54.	I get instructions from different people working above me on budget matters	......	......	......	......	......
55.	The setting of my budget goals is pretty much under my control	......	......	......	......	......
56.	Assistance from staff department is available on budget matters with little persuation	......	......	......	......	......
57.	Seniors tend to tell and demand in preference to ask or persuade on budget matters	......	......	......	......	......
58.	Budget evaluation does not concern with 'human considerations'	......	......	......	......	......
59.	I am very clear about the limits of authority in my present position	......	......	......	......	......
60.	I have complete control over the means of reaching my budget targets	......	......	......	......	......
61.	I discuss budget items with staff whenever occurs without hesitation	......	......	......	......	......
62.	My seniors join us in developing department's goals and priorities	......	......	......	......	......
63.	My seniors are never satisfied with my explanation of budget variances in my department	......	......	......	......	......
64.	I am very clear about the expectations of people around me	......	......	......	......	......
65.	Staff advice is very useful in achieving budget standards	......	......	......	......	......
66.	Seniors enjoy free and frank dialogue with subordinates on budget matters	......	......	......	......	......
67.	Seniors encourage free flow of information and ideas among					

group members	......	......	......	......	......
68. I enjoyed participating in this research project	......	......	......	......	......

REFERENCES

(1). Anthony, R., *Managerial Accounting,* Homewood, III., Irwin, 1960: 68.

(2). Johnson, F., Alienation: An Overview and Introduction, *In Alienation: Concepts, Terms, and Meanings,* edited by Frank Johnson, New York, Seminar Press, 1973: 3-25.

(3). Seeman, M., The Urban Alienation: Some Dubicious Theses from Marx to Marcuse: *Journal of Personality and Social Psychology,* 19: 1971: 135-43.

(4). Johnson, F., Alienation: Concepts, Term and World: *In Alienation: Concepts, Terms and Meanings,* edited by Frank Johnson, New York, Seminar Press, 1973: 27-51.

(5). Jenkins, D., *Job Power,* New York: Doubleday, 1973: 43.

(6). Tocqueville, Alexis de., *Democracy in America,* Vol. 2, New York: Shocken Books, 1961: 190-91.

(7). Argyris, C., *The Impact of Budgets on People.* Ithaca, School of Business and Public Administration, Cornell University, 1952: 25.

(8). Peirce, J.L., The Budget Comes of Age, *Harvard Business Review,* Vol.32, No.3, May, 1954 : 58-66.

(9). Irvine, V.B., Budgeting - Funcitional Analysis and Behavioural Implications, *Cost Management,* March-April, 1970: 6-16.

(10). Milton, F.U., Solving the Problems of Human Relations in Budgeting, *Budgeting,* 16 Nov.-Dec., 1968: 4-6.

(11). Hofstede, G.H., *The Game of Budget Control.* Tavistock, London, 1968.

(12). Cook, T.D., and D.T. Campbell, The Design and Conduct of Quasi-experiments and True Experiments in Field-Settings, Chapter 7 in M.D. Dunnette, *Handbook of Industrial and Organisational Psychology*. Chicago: Rand McNally, 1976: 223-326.

(13). DeCoster, D.T. and J.P., Fertakis, Budget-Induced Pressure and its Relationship to Supervisory Behavior. *Journal of Accounting Research*, Vol. 6, No. 2, Autumn, 1968: 237-246.

(14). Schiff, M., and A.Y. Lewin, Where Traditional Budgeting Fails, *Financial Executive*, 36, 1968: 50-52, 55-56 and 61-62.

- The Impact of People on Budget, *Accounting Review,* 15: 1970: 259-268.

(15). Onsi, M., Factor Analysis of Behavioral Variables Affecting Budgetary Slack, *Accounting Review,* XLVIII: 1973: 535-548.

(16). Hopwood, A.G., An Empirical Study of the Role of Accounting Data in Performance Evaluation, Empirical Research in Accounting, Selected Studies, 1972, Supplement to the *Journal of Accounting Research,* 1972: 156-182.

(17). Swieringa, R.J., and R.H. Moncur, The Relationship between Manager's Budget-Oriented Behaviour and Selected Attitude, Position, Size and Performance Measures, Empirical Research in Accounting: Selected Studies, 1972, Supplement to the *Journal of Accounting Research, 1972:* 194-205.

(18). Kenis, I., Effects of Budgetary Goal Characteristics on Managerial Attitudes and Performance. *The Accounting Review,* October, 1979: 707-721.

(19). Bruns, W.J., Jr., and J.H. Waterhouse, Budgetary Control and Organisation Structure, *Journal of Accounting Research,* Autumn, 1975: 177-203.

(20). Macintosh, N.B., Differing Attitudes to Budgetary Control: Organisational Implications, *Costs and Management*, Jan-Feb, 1983: 19-24.

(21). Merchant, K.A., The Design of the Corporate Budgeting System: Influences on Managerial Behaviour and Performance, *The Accounting Review,* October, 1981: 813-829.

(22). Heneman, H.G., Comparisions of Self and Superior Ratings of Managerial Performance, *Journal of Applied Psychology,* October, 1974: 638-642.

(23). Hackman, J.R., and L.W. Porter, Expectancy Theory Predictions of Work Effectiveness, *Organisational Behaviour and Human Performance,* November 1980: 417-426.

(24). Dermer, J.D., The Interrelationship of Intrinsic and Extrinsic Motivation, *Academy of Management Journal,* March, 1975: 125-129.

(25). Harman, H.H., *Modern Factor Analysis,* Chicago; Universtiy of Chicago, 1967: 311.

(26). Thurstone, L.L., *Multiple Factor Analysis,* Chicago: University of Cicago Press, 1947: 299-300, 318.

(27). Harris, C.W., Some Recent Developments in Factor Analysis. *Educational and Psychological Measurement* 24: 1964: 193-206.

(28). Kaiser, H.F., The Varimax Criterion for Analytic Rotation in Factor Aalysis, *Psychometrica:* 23: 1958: 187-200.

(29). Warburton, F.W., Analytic Methods of Factor Rotation. *British Journal of Statistical Psychology* 16: 1963: 165-7.

(30). Simon, H.A., H. Guetzkow, G. Kozmetsky and G. Tyndall *Centralisation vs Decentralisation in Organising the Controller's Department,* Controllership Foundation, Inc., New York, 1954: 3-4.

(31). Stedry, A.C., *Budget Control and Cost Behaviour,* Englewood Cliffs, N.J., Prentice-Hall, Inc., 1960.

(32). DeCoster, D.T., and J.P. Fertakis, Induced-Budget Pressure and its Relationship to Supervisory Behaviour *Journal of Accounting Research,* 6, 1968: 237-46.

(33). Holstrum, G.L., The Effect of Budget Adaptiveness and Tightness on Managerial Decision Making, *Journal of Accounting Research,* Vol.9, No.2, Autumn, 1971: 268-77.

(34). Bernard, A., Non-businessman as Surrogates for Businessman in Behavioural Research, *Journal of Business,* XL: April 1967: 203-207.

(35). Cherrington, D.T. and J.O. Cherrington, Appropriate Reinforcement Contingencies in the Budgeting Process, Empirical Research in Accounting: Selected Studies: Supplement to the *Journal of Accounting Research,* 1973: 225-253.

(36). Becker, S.W., Discussion of Appropriate Reinforcemnt Contingencies in the Budget Process: Empirical Research in Accounting: Selected Studies: Supplement to the *Journal of Accounting Research,* 1973: 254-256.

(37). Hofstedt, T.R., Discussion of Appropriate Reinforcement

Contingencies in the Budget Process: Empirical Research in Accounting : Selected Studies: Supplement to the *Journal of Accounting Research,* 1973: 257-266.

(38). Collins, F., The Interaction of Budget Characteristics and Personality Variables with Budgetary Response Attitudes, *The Accounting Review,* Vol. LIII, No.3, April 1978: 324-335.

(39). Brownell, P., Participation in Budgeting, Locus of Control and Organisational Effectiveness, *The Accounting Review,* Vol. LVI, No.4., October 1981: 844-860.

(40). Kohler, E.L., *A Dictionary For Accountants,* Englewood Cliffs, N.J., Prentice-Hall, Inc., 1957: 75.

(41). Mey, A., Bedrijfsbergroting en Bedrijfsbeleid, *Leiden,* Stenfert Kroese, N.V., 1951.

(42). Homer, A.B., J.E. Champion and R. Gene Brown, *Accounting in Business Decisions: Theroy, Method and Use*, 2nd ed., Englewood Cliffs, N.J., Prentice-Hall, Inc., 1967: 719.

(43). Willemze, F.G., Under the influence of accountant the main stress has often been put on accountability and making people responsible. This means that more attention was paid to the function than to the functioning, Kwaliteitsbeleid en Industriele Organisatie Morgen, *Statistica Neerlandica,* 1964: 2: 189-200.

(44). Youmann, E.G., The Administrative Mind, *Public Personnel Review,* Vol.15, No.2, April 1954: 72-76.

(45). Moore, J.F., Too Much Management, Too Little Change, *Harvard Business Review,* Vol.35, Jan-Feb, 1956: 41-49.

(46). Argyris, C., and F.B. Miller, *The Impact of Budgets on People:* Controllership Foundation, Inc., New York, 1962: 16.

(47). Argyris, C. and T. Graham, The Member-Centered Conference as a Research Method, II, *Human Organisation,* Vol. 10, No. 1, Spring 1951: 22-27.
Personnel Journal, Vol.33, No. 1, May 1954:3.

(48). Newman, M.H. and J.P. Logan, *Management of Expanding Enterprises.* New York: Columbia University Press, 1955: 55.

(49). Martin, V., Self-examination for Progressive Management, *Occupational Papers in Management.* Industrial Relations Center, University of Chicago: No.7, November 1955: 5-6.

(50). Hodges, H.G., *Management,* Boston: Houghton Miffin, 1956: 162.

(51). Wallace, M.E., Behavioral Considerations in Budgeting,

Management Accounting, Vol. 47, No.12, August 1966: 3-8.

(52). Abruzzi, A., Formulating a Theroy of Work Management, *Management Science*, Vol. 2, No.2, January 1956: 114-130.

(53). Jasinski, F., Use and Misuse of Efficiency Controls, *Harvard Business Review*, July-August, 1956.

(54). Lewin, K. et. al., Level of Aspiration in J. Mc V. Hunt (ed.) *Personality Behaviour & Disorders*, Ronald Press, New York, 1944: 333-378.

(55). Robert, C.H., The System vs. the Man, *Budgeting*, May-June 1967: 10.

(56). Roy, E.C. Marshall, Human Problems in Budgeting, *The Australian Accountant*, August 1971: 305-6.

(57). Amey, L.R. and D.A. Egginton, *Management Accounting: A Conceptual Approach*, Longman, London, 1973: 562.

(58). Shillinglaw, G., Divisional Performance Review: An Extension of Budgetary Control, Chapter 8 in Bonini, C.P., R.K. Jaedicke and H.M. Wagner, eds., *Management Controls:* New Directions in Basic Research, McGraw-Hill, New York, 1964.

(59). Shubik, M., The Uses of Game Theory in Management Science; *Management Science*, 2, 1955: 40-54.

(60). Luce, R.D. and H. Raiffa: *Games and Decisions: Introduction and Critical Survey* (Wiley, New York, 1967).

(61). Marschak, J., Elements for a Theroy of Teams: *Management Science*, 1, 1955: 127-137.

(62). Drever, J., A *Dictionary of Psychology*, London, Penguin Reference Books, 1952: 103 and 211.

(63). Vajda, S., *An Introduction to Linear Programming and the Theroy of Games*, London/New York, Methuen & Co./John Wiley and Sons, 1960.

(64). Berne, E., *Games People Play*: The Psychology of Human Relationships, London, Andre Deutsch, 1966.
The Intimacy Experiment, *Transactional Analysis Bulletin*, 3, 1964: 113.

(65). Potter, S., *The Theory and Practice of Gamesmanship*, Harmonds Worth, Penguin Books, 1962: 10.

(66). Valentine, C.S., *The Psychology of Early Childhood*, Mathuen, London, 1942.

(67). Heckhausen, H. and G. Seibt, An Fange und Entwicklung der Leistungs-Motivation: III, Im Freien Spiel des K Leinkindes. *Psychol. Forsch:* 669.

(68). Chateav, J., L' enfant et le jeu. *Scarabes,* Paris, 1967.

(69). Huizinga, J., *Homo Ludens,* A Study of the Play Element in Culture. London Routledge and Kigal Paul, 1949: 26.

(70). Piaget, J., *Play, Dreams and Imitations in Childhood.* New York, Norton, 1951.

(71). Baldwin, J.M., Play: *Dictionary of Philosophy & Psychology,* 1960: 303.

(72). Anthony., S., *Creativity and Play:* The Dynamics of Creation: 113.

(73). Buhler, K., *The Mental Development of the Child.* Harcourt Brace, New York, 1930.

(74). Berlyne, D.E., *Conflict, Arousal* and *Curiosity,* New York: Mc-Graw Hill, 1960.

(75). Coch, L. and J.R.P. French Jr., Overcoming Resistance to Change, *Human Relations,* London, 1948, Vol.I: 512-32.

(76). Fraser, J.M., Human Relation in a Fully Employed Democracy, London, Sir Isaac Pitman and Sons Ltd. 1960: 195-96.

(77). Beinum, H.J. Van, Een Organisatie in Beweging, *Leiden, Slenfert* Kroese, 1963.

Sociatrie Van de Arbeid, *Assen,* Van Gorcum, 1966: 12.

(78). Hutte, H.A., Decision-Taking in Management Game, *Human Relations,* London, Vol. I, 1965: 5-20.

(79). Klein, L., Rationality in Management Control, *The Journal of Management Studies,* Oxford, Vol.3, 1965: 351-361.

(80). Vroom, V.H., Some Personality Determinants of the Effects of Participation: *The Journal of Abnormal and Social Psychology,* 3, 1959: 322-327.

(81). French, J.R.P. Jr., J. Israel and D. As, An Experiment on Participation in a Norwegian Factory: Interpersonal Dimensions of Decision-making, *Human Relations,* London, Vol. 13, 1960: 3-20.

(82). Colen, J.P., Cooper and P. Thorne, A Note on Communication in a Factory, *Occupational Psychology,* London, I, 1965, 25-30.

(83). Carr, A.Z., *Business as a Game:* The Macmillan Company of India Ltd., Delhi, 1972.

(84). Tovey, D.E., *The Accountant's Role in Budgeting,* Lausanne, Unpublished Participants Paper of IMEDE, 1963.

(85). Fuyuume, J., Working with Operating Management, *NAA*

Bulletin, Management Accounting, 1965: 51-57.

(86). Mc Gregor, D., *The Human Side of Enterprise:* Mc Graw-Hill Book Company, Inc., New York, 1960.

(87). Likert, R., *New Patterns of Management,* New York, McGraw Hill, 1961.

(88). March, J.G. and H.A. Simon, *Organisations,* New York, John Wiley & Sons, 1958: 126.

(89). Gamson, W.A. and Norman A.S., Scapegoating in Baseball, *American Journal of Sociology,* 70, 1964, 69-72.

(90). Pym, D., Effective Managerial Performance in Organisational Change, *The Journal of Management Studies I,* 1966: 73-84.

(91). Bennis, W.G., Revisionist Theory of Leadership, *Harvard Business Review,* I, 1961: 26-34.

(92). Levin, K., T. Dembo, L. Festinger and Sears: Level of Aspiration, in J. McV. Hunt (ed.), *Personality and Behavior Disorders,* Vol.I, Ronald Press, New York, 1944: 333-78.

(93). Bayton, J.A., Interrelations Between Levels of Aspiration, Performance and Estimates of Past Performance, *Journal of Experimental Psychology,* Vol.33, 1943: 1-21.

(94). Becker, S.W. and D. Green Jr., Budgeting and Employee Behaviour, *Journal of Business,* Vol. 35, No.4, October 1962: 392-402.

(95). Cook, D.M., The Effect of Frequency of Feedback on Attitudes and Performance: Empirical Research in Accounting: Selected Studies, Supplement to Vol. 5 of *Journal of Accounting Research,* 1967: 221.

(96). Child, J.L. and J.W.M. Whiting; Determinants of Level of Aspiration: Evidence from Everyday Life, in H. Brand (ed.), *The Study of Personality,* John Wiley & Sons Inc., New York, 1954: 145-58.

(97). Fryer, E.W., *An Evaluation of Level of Aspiration in a Training Procedure,* Englewood Cliffs, N.J., Prentice Hall, 1963.

(98). Locke, E.A. and J.F. Bryan, The Directing Function of Goals in Task Performance, *Organisational Behaviour and Human Performance,* 4, 1969: 35-42.

(99). Stedry, A.C. and E. Kay., The Effects of Goal Difficulty on Performance, A Field Experiment, Publication of Sloan School of Management, M.I.T., Cambridge (Mass), 1964.

(100). Davis, K., *Human Relations at Work*, New York, McGraw-Hill, 1962.

(101). French, J.R.P. Jr., E. kay Jr. and H.H. Meyer, *A Study of Threat and Participation in a Performance Appraisal Situation*, General Electrical Co., New York, 1962.

(102). Steers, R.M., Task Goal Attributes, An Achievement and Supervisory Performance, *Organisational Behaviour and Human Performance,* 1975: 392-403.

(103). Milani, K., The Relationship of Participation in Budget -Setting to Industrial Supervisor Performance and Attitudes: A Field Study. *Accounting Review,* April 1975: 274-284.

(104). Likert, R.A., Motivational Approach to a Modified Theory of Organisation and Management. In Haire, M. (ed.) *Modern Organisation Theroy,* John Wiley, New York, 1959: 184-217.

(105). Kahn, D., N. Maccoby and N. Morse, *Productivity, Supervision and Morale in an Office Situation.* Ann Arbor: University of Michigan, Institute for Social Research, 1950.

(106). Katz, D., N. Maccoby, G. Gurin and L.G. Floor, *Productivity Supervision and Morale Among Railroad Workers:* Ann Arbor: University of Michigan, Survey Research Center, Institute for Social Research, 1951.

(107). White, R. and Lippitt, Leader Behavior and Member Reaction in Three Social Climates, in Dorwin Cartwright and Alwin Zander: *Group Dynamics,* Evanston, Row, Peterson 1960: 327-53.

(108). Kahn., R.L. and D. Katz, Leadership Practices in Relation to Productivity and Morale, in D. Cartwright and A. Zander (eds.) *Group Dynamics,* 2nd ed., Row Peterson & Co., Evanston, III, 1960: 527-53.

(109). Hartmann, G.W. and T. Newcomb (eds.), *Industrial Conflict,* New York: Gorden.

(110). Colenan, C .J., Avoiding the Pitfalls in Results-oriented Appraisals: *Personnel,* Nov.- Dec., 1965: 24.

(111). Ammons, R., Effects of Knowledge of Performance: A Survey and Tentative Theoretical Formulation. *Journal of Genetic Psychology,* 54, 1956: 279-299.

(112). Pryer, M.W. and B.M. Bass, Some Effects of Feedback on Behavior in Groups, *Sociometry,* 22, 1959: 56-63.

(113). Zajonc, R.B., The Effects of Feedback and Group Task Difficulty on Individual and Group Performance, *Technical Report 15,* Contract NONR 1224(34). Ann Arbor, Michigan, University of Michigan, 1961.

(114). Smith, E.E., and S.S. Knight, Effects of Feedback on Insight and Problem-solving Efficiency in Traininig Groups, *Journal of Applied Psychology,* 43, 1959: 209-211.

(115). Weitz, J.A., J. Antoinette and S.R. Wallace, The Effect of Home Office Contact on Sales Performance, *Personnel Psychology,* 7, 1954: 381-84.

(116). Miller, L., *The Use of Knowledge of Results in Improving the Performance of Hourly Operators,* General Electrical Company. Behavioral Research Service, 1965.

(117). Hundal, P.S., Knowledge of Performance as an Incentive in Respective Industrial Work: *Journal of Applied Psychology,* 53, 1969: 224-226.

(118). French, E.G., Effects of the Interaction of Feedback and Motivation on Task Performance, *American Psychologist,* 11, 1965: 395 (abstract).

(119). Leavitt, H.J. and R.A.H. Mueller, Some Effects of Feedback on Communication, *Human Relations*, Vol.4, 1951: 401-10.

(120). Hamblin, R.L. and J.A. Wiggins, Ambiguity and the Rate of Social Adaptation, *Technical Report-I,* Contract ONR 811(16). St. Louis: Washington University, 1959.

(121). Smith, E.E., The Effect of Clear and Unclear Role Expectations on Group Productivity and Defensiveness, *Journal of Abnormal and Social Psychology,* 55, 1957: 213-217.

(122). Kay, E., H.H. Meyer and J.R.P. French, Jr., The Effect of Threat in a Performance Appraisal Interview, *Journal of Applied Psychology,* 49, 1965: 311-317.

(123). Woodward, J., *Industrial Organisation: Theory and Practice* Oxford University Press, 1965.

(124). Burns, T. and G.M. Stalker, *The Management of Innovation* Tavistock, 1968.

(125). Lawrence, P.R. and J.W. Lorsch, *Organisation and Environment:* Managing Differentiation and Integration. Harvard University, 1967.

(126). Pugh, D.J., J.R. Hickson, C.R. Hinings and G. Turner, Dimensions of Organisation Structure, *Administrative Science Quarterly,* June, 1968: 65-105.

(127). Worthy, J.C., Organisational Structure and Employee Morale, *American Sociological Review,* Vol. 15, 1950: 173.

(128). Marriott, R., Size of the Working Group and Output, *Occupational Psychology,* Vol.23, 1949: 47-57.

(129). Whitin, T.M., On the Span of Central Direction, *Naval Research Logistics Quarterly,* Vol. 1, 1954: 27.
(130). Chaplin, F.S., J. Etsouderous: Formalisation Observed in Ten Voluntary Associations: *Concepts, Morphology, and Process and Social Forces,* Vol.33, 1955: 306-309.
(131). Pugh, D.S., D.J. Hickson, C.R. Hinings and C. Turner, The Context of Organisation Structure, *Administrative Science Quarterly,* March, 1969: 91-114.
(132). Child, J., Organisation Structure, Environment and Performance: The Role of Strategic Choice, *Sociology,* January 1972: 1-22.
(133). Perrow, C., A Framework for the Comparative Analysis of Organisations, *American Sociological Review,* April, 1967: 194-208.
(134). U.S. Department of Labour: *Job Performance and Age: A Study of Measurement,* Washington D.C. Government Printing Office, Bureau of Labour Statistics, Bulletin No. 1203, 1956.
(135). Maher, H., Age and Performance of Two Work Groups: *Journal of Gerontology,* 10, 1955: 448-451.
(136). Bowers, W., An Appraisal of Worker Characteristics as Related to Age: *Journal of Applied Psychology,* 36, 1952: 296-300.
(137). Uhrbrock, R.S., Attitudes of 4430 Employees. *Journal of Social Psychology,* 5, 1934: 365-372.
(138). Wyatt, S., J.N. Langdon and F. Stock, Fatigue and Boredom in Repetitive Work: *Industrial Health and Research* Board (London), Rep., 77, 1937.
(139). Kornhauser, A.W., and A.A. Sharp, Employee Attitudes: Suggestions from a Study in a Factory, *Personnel Journal,* 10, 1932: 393-404.
(140). Hoppock, R., *Job Satisfaction:* New York: Harper & Brothers, 1935.
(141). Fortune Magazine, May 1937: 5.
(142). Raube, S.A., the Problem of Boredom, Conference Board Management Record, 10, December 1948: 565-75.
(143). Vitels, M.S., Man and Machine Relationship - The Problem of Boredom, Proceedings of 1950, *Annual Fall Conference, Society for Advancement of Management,* New York, 1951: 129-38.
(144). Walker, C.R., The Problem of the Repetitive Job, *Harvard*

Business Review, 28, 3, 1950: 54-58.

(145). Walker, C.R. and H.R. Guest, The Man on the Assembly Line, *Harvard Business Review,* 30, 3, 1952: 71-83.

(146). Burns, C.P., *The Philosophy of Labour:* Allen & Unwin Ltd., 1925.

(147). Gurin, G., J. Veroff and S. Feld., *American View: Their Mental Health,* New York: Basic Books Inc. 1960.

(148). Herzberg, F., B. Mausner, R.O. Peterson and D.F. Capwell, *Job Attitudes: Review of Research and Opinion.* Pittsburghs Psychological Service of Pittsburgh, 1957.

Index